SpringerBriefs in Economics

AF183833

SpringerBriefs present concise summaries of cutting-edge research and practical applications across a wide spectrum of fields. Featuring compact volumes of 50 to 125 pages, the series covers a range of content from professional to academic. Typical topics might include:

- A timely report of state-of-the art analytical techniques
- A bridge between new research results, as published in journal articles, and a contextual literature review
- A snapshot of a hot or emerging topic
- An in-depth case study or clinical example
- A presentation of core concepts that students must understand in order to make independent contributions

SpringerBriefs in Economics showcase emerging theory, empirical research, and practical application in microeconomics, macroeconomics, economic policy, public finance, econometrics, regional science, and related fields, from a global author community.

Briefs are characterized by fast, global electronic dissemination, standard publishing contracts, standardized manuscript preparation and formatting guidelines, and expedited production schedules.

David Mendoza-Tinoco
Alfonso Mercado-Garcia • Dabo Guan

Multiregional Flood Footprint Analysis

An Appraisal of the Economic Impact of Flooding Events

Springer

David Mendoza-Tinoco
Faculty of Economics
Universidad Autonoma de Coahuila
Coahuila, Coahuila, Mexico

Alfonso Mercado-Garcia
Programme of Interdisciplinary Studies
El Colegio de Mexico
Tlalpan, Mexico

Dabo Guan
Department of Earth System Science
Tsinghua University
Beijing, China

ISSN 2191-5504 ISSN 2191-5512 (electronic)
SpringerBriefs in Economics
ISBN 978-3-031-29727-4 ISBN 978-3-031-29728-1 (eBook)
https://doi.org/10.1007/978-3-031-29728-1

© The Editor(s) (if applicable) and The Author(s), under exclusive license to Springer Nature Switzerland AG 2023
This work is subject to copyright. All rights are solely and exclusively licensed by the Publisher, whether the whole or part of the material is concerned, specifically the rights of translation, reprinting, reuse of illustrations, recitation, broadcasting, reproduction on microfilms or in any other physical way, and transmission or information storage and retrieval, electronic adaptation, computer software, or by similar or dissimilar methodology now known or hereafter developed.
The use of general descriptive names, registered names, trademarks, service marks, etc. in this publication does not imply, even in the absence of a specific statement, that such names are exempt from the relevant protective laws and regulations and therefore free for general use.
The publisher, the authors, and the editors are safe to assume that the advice and information in this book are believed to be true and accurate at the date of publication. Neither the publisher nor the authors or the editors give a warranty, expressed or implied, with respect to the material contained herein or for any errors or omissions that may have been made. The publisher remains neutral with regard to jurisdictional claims in published maps and institutional affiliations.

This Springer imprint is published by the registered company Springer Nature Switzerland AG
The registered company address is: Gewerbestrasse 11, 6330 Cham, Switzerland

Acknowledgments

Various parts of this book were enriched by discussions and suggestions in various specialized seminars. Also, some case studies of the book had the financial support of the European Commission (Directorate-General for Climate Action within the project CLIMA.C.3/SER/2013/0019) and the UK Engineering and Physical Sciences Research Council (EP/K013661/1). The research also had the financial support from the Mexican National Council of Science and Technology, with the doctorate scholarship Num. 311512. Our gratitude also to Terry Bohn for her English editing of this book and to Dr. Jun Li for his support in the software coding.

Contents

List of Figures

List of Table

Chapter 1
Introduction

This book proposes an appraisal methodology for the direct and indirect costs of the effects of natural disasters in a particular region and the resulting cascading events which follow in the multiregional/global scope. The evaluation of these costs constitutes the Multiregional Flood Footprint Assessment (MFFA). The term "natural" disaster is used in the sense of a natural hazard that significantly harms a community and might be a man-accelerated natural event (Gould et al. 2016), for example, an earthquake, a flood, a heat wave, a hurricane, or a volcanic eruption.

The book provides a detailed description of the methodology used to construct the MFFA and a series of case studies to test the feasibility of the proposed models. The proposed assessment is useful for understanding how an economic shock is transmitted and propagated to wider economic systems and social networks, generating additional indirect economic costs. It is based on the input-output economic framework and further develops a previous single-regional Flood Footprint Model towards the multiregional dimension. Its objective is twofold: (a) to estimate the direct costs to each economic sector or industry based on the information provided by different estimation methods for flood damages to physical assets and (b) to estimate secondary effects, considering the economic mechanisms that affect the production in industries and regions economically linked with sectors in the affected region. The evidence provided by case studies points out the need to develop global adaptation strategies, allocating resources for climate risk management in those vulnerable regions that, if impacted by a disaster, would trigger severe indirect costs to other countries.

The remainder of this book is composed as follows. Chapter 2 reviews the most widely used methods to calculate the costs of a disaster. In Chap. 3, a MFFA is proposed, developing a single-regional Flood Footprint Model and extending it towards a multiregional model. Chapter 4 presents four empirical case studies and applies the proposed MFFA to the last of these cases, a hypothetical flooding event in the city of Rotterdam. This chapter shows how the consequences of an extreme climate event in a city affect the national economy and how these disruptions propagate worldwide through its economic interconnections. Finally, Chap. 5 summarises the main conclusions of the book.

© The Author(s), under exclusive license to Springer Nature Switzerland AG 2023

D. Mendoza-Tinoco et al., *Multiregional Flood Footprint Analysis*, SpringerBriefs in Economics, https://doi.org/10.1007/978-3-031-29728-1_1

Chapter 2
Theoretical and Methodological Background

2.1 Introduction

The assessment of disaster costs is particularly difficult. How does one combine, for example, the destruction of a cultural heritage building with the loss of human lives or with the destruction of a house? Concerning the secondary effects of destruction, how does one quantify radiation pollution from damages to a nuclear reactor, or the loss in productivity because a factory outside of the impacted region cannot get necessary inputs from an affected factory on the other side of the world?

The estimation of total costs of a disaster, including the costs of destruction directly caused by the disaster and the costs of secondary effects from such destruction, presents two main difficulties. Firstly, it is practically impossible to account for all dimensions of the damages (e.g. casualties or destroyed biodiversity). Secondly, even when there are some attempts to quantify the damages, it would be extremely complex and biased to combine these damages into a single unit. Despite these limitations, such an economic appraisal presents some benefits in that it provides an overview of the damages, which is useful for risk management strategic planning (Cochrane 2004; Sahin and Yavuz 2015).

Important applied research on the economic impact of disasters has been produced. Traditionally, the evaluation of direct economic damages has been used to provide an approximate overview of such damages (Crowther et al. 2007; Rose 2004). Another research line has been focused on the appraisal of the indirect economic costs caused by a disaster (Okuyama 2009; Rose 2004; Lazzaroni and van Bergeijk 2014; Veen 2004). Furthermore, some authors (Hallegatte and Przyluski 2010; Okuyama 2009) have pointed out the existence of other kinds of costs rarely considered in disaster impact analyses, which they refer to as general equilibrium costs, which usually only become visible in the long run.

Theoretical content in this section is mainly based on Miller and Blair (2009).

© The Author(s), under exclusive license to Springer Nature Switzerland AG 2023
D. Mendoza-Tinoco et al., *Multiregional Flood Footprint Analysis*, SpringerBriefs in Economics, https://doi.org/10.1007/978-3-031-29728-1_2

The economic techniques most widely used in the appraisal of damages include extensions of input-output (IO) analysis, computable general equilibrium (CGE) models, econometric techniques, social accountability matrices, survey-based analyses, and hybrid methods.

Among these, IO analyses and CGE models (and their extensions) are the most widely used in the research on economic impact analysis. In general, we can say that the estimations from IO analysis are usually seen as the upper-bound estimation, while estimations from CGE models are commonly taken as the lower bound, or "optimistic" estimation (Okuyama 2007, 2009; Rose 2004; Koks et al. 2016a; Zhou and Chen 2021). Another distinction is that the estimations from IO models are regarded as short-term costs as prices stay rigid, while estimations from CGE models can be considered as long-term costs when prices are flexible (Koks et al. 2016a, b; Galbusera and Giannopoulos 2018). As an average solution, some authors (Hallegatte and Przyluski 2010) have suggested the use of hybrid (IO-CGE) models. Nevertheless, they are highly data intensive and depend on a large number of parameters, many of which are user-calibrated (Cochrane 1997; Okuyama 2003).

Some researchers (Cole 2003; Li et al. 2013; Okuyama 2007; Rose 2004; Galbusera and Giannopoulos 2018; Triple E Consulting 2014) found that IO models (and their ad hoc extensions) are more widely used than CGE models. **They argue that this is mainly based on the possibilities of IO modelling to deal with the various aspects involved in assessing the economic impact of a disaster, especially the relevant capacity of** accounting for economic imbalances in a disaster aftermath, **along with the advantages of applying the parsimony principle and transparent results with the possibility of regional and industry-sectoral analysis** (Li et al. 2013).

IO analysis was originally developed by the Nobel Prize laureate economist Wassily Leontief in the 1930s. The main strength of IO models is the representation in an elegant and straightforward way of the complex interconnectedness and the flows of goods and services among different economic agents. This analysis departs from the basic economic theory of the circular flow of the economy. The information is accommodated in IO tables, which account for the inter-industrial[1] transactions (sales and purchase), final demand, and payment for productive factors, normally depicted as the value added of the sector.[2]

Included in the modelling adaptations for impact analysis are a consideration of the economy's disequilibrium, supply bottlenecks, product substitution, changes in intermediate and final demand, and the time dynamics of the recovery (Cole 2003; Okuyama 2007, 2009; Rose 2004; Veen 2004). The research on impact analysis in IO models has shown great dynamism in recent years, which promises further

[1] Hereinafter, the term "industry" can be interpreted equivalently with the terms 'economic sector', and 'industrial sector'.

[2] See a classical theoretical explanation and its mathematical development in Miller and Blair (2009).

development and refinement of the modelling (Okuyama and Santos 2014; Rose 2004; Veen 2004; Galbusera and Giannopoulos 2018; Sun et al. 2020).

Owing to the aforementioned reasons, the methodological development in this book is based upon the IO approach. Therefore, the following sections expand upon its environmental extensions and its applications to disasters.

	Inter-industry transactions	**Final demand**	**Total output**
	$\begin{bmatrix} z_{11} & \cdots & z_{1j} & \cdots & z_{1n} \\ \vdots & \ddots & \vdots & \ddots & \vdots \\ z_{i1} & \cdots & z_{ij} & \cdots & z_{in} \\ \vdots & \ddots & \vdots & \ddots & \vdots \\ z_{n1} & \cdots & z_{nj} & \cdots & z_{nn} \end{bmatrix}$	$\begin{bmatrix} f_1 \\ \vdots \\ f_i \\ \vdots \\ f_n \end{bmatrix}$	$\begin{bmatrix} x_1 \\ \vdots \\ x_i \\ \vdots \\ x_n \end{bmatrix}$
Value added	$[va_1 + \cdots + va_j + \cdots + va_n]$		
Total inputs	$[x_1 + \cdots + x_j + \cdots + x_n]$		

2.2 Applications of Standard IO Analysis to Disasters

It is not common to find academic research with direct applications of standard IO analysis to the estimation of the economic losses from a disaster due to the characteristics of disasters, and there is a need to adapt the modelling to overcome some original rigidities in standard IO analysis to make it suitable for impact assessment. Nevertheless, when the necessity of having prompt answers to formulate a general assessment of damage exists, particularly in specific cases where a sectorial *radiography* of the economy after a disaster is needed, standard IO analysis becomes a useful tool. This was the case after Hurricane Sandy affected the East Coast of North America. To make a prompt estimation of indirect costs to help in the planning of recovery strategies, the Natural Hazard and Earth System Sciences (NHESS) conducted an analysis of damages on the different sectors of the US economy using a standard IO model. Most of the damages were felt by the chemical and textile industries. The analysis assumed an average disruption (power shortage) of 2 days, which affected around 26.5% of the manufacturing sectors. This analysis was made to assess the effects of disruptions in what can be considered critical infrastructure (i.e. that on which many sectors depend). They estimated the indirect damages to be US $9.4 billion (Kunz et al. 2013).

Another application of standard IO analysis was in the development of the inoperability input-output model (IIOM) developed by Santos (2006). In the IIOM, *inoperability* is defined as the difference between the planned output of an economy and the level of output that the system can produce after a negative shock. Based on this concept, the IIOM assumes a direct relationship between the value of transactions and the interdependency between economic sectors. Then, the matrix of technical coefficients ($\boldsymbol{A}$) is transformed into a matrix where the coefficients represent the strength of the relationship between sectors ($\boldsymbol{A}^*$), where each element $[a^*_{ij}]$ indicates the inoperability in sector i attributable to disruptions in sector j. It must be noted that the original IIOM is a demand-driven and static model where equilibrium is assumed at each step (Santos and Haimes 2004). Despite its criticised rigidities, the IIOM has proved useful in assessing inoperability among economic sectors, which has helped in taking actions to prepare for, or mitigate, adverse impacts from negative shocks by identifying which sectors are the most vulnerable (Crowther et al. 2007).

2.2.1 Supply IO Model: The Ghosh Model

From the development of a demand-driven model, Ghosh (1958) proposed an alternative model to relate the production of each sector with the supply of primary inputs, such as the labour force. Mathematically, this model proposes to divide the elements in row i by the correspondent industrial gross product of sector i (x_i), instead of each element in a column j, divided by its industrial gross product (x_j). This process generates the matrix $\boldsymbol{B}$:

$$\boldsymbol{B} = \widehat{\boldsymbol{x}}^{-1}\boldsymbol{Z}. \tag{2.1}$$

All elements of matrix $\boldsymbol{B}$, $[b_{ij}]$, are usually referred to as *allocation* coefficients, as they express the proportion of sales of sector i to all industries j. From the above expression and given the fact that $\boldsymbol{x}' = \boldsymbol{i}'\boldsymbol{Z} + \boldsymbol{v}'$, we can obtain an expression where the production of each sector becomes a function of the primary inputs. This process is analogous to the one to obtain the *input inverse* (Leontief inverse matrix):

$$\begin{aligned} \boldsymbol{x}' &= \boldsymbol{i}'\widehat{\boldsymbol{x}}^{-1}\boldsymbol{Z} + \boldsymbol{v}' \\ &= \boldsymbol{x}'\boldsymbol{B} + \boldsymbol{v}' \\ &= \boldsymbol{v}'(\boldsymbol{I} - \boldsymbol{B})^{-1} \\ &= \boldsymbol{v}'\boldsymbol{G} \end{aligned} \tag{2.2}$$

where $\boldsymbol{G}$ is named as the *output inverse* matrix and whose elements $[g_{ij}]$ represent the total change in the value of output in sector j from a change of one unit in the availability of the *primary inputs* from sector i. As previously stated, we can obtain the relationship in changes:

$$\Delta x' = (\Delta v')G \tag{2.3}$$

Similar to the interpretation of column and row sums in the quantity model (the Leontief model), the row sums in the Ghosh model can be thought of as the *input multipliers* that show the effect on total output in the economy of a change of one unit of value in the supply of primary inputs from industry *i*. In an analogue way, the column sum of elements in $\boldsymbol{G}$ gives the total effect on the output of industry *j* from the change of one-unit value in the supply of primary factors in each industry. It can be noted that the information provided from the *input multipliers* can be applied for the best allocation of additional primary inputs among industries to maximise the increase of output in the economy (the opposite is also true regarding the potential reduction in output from shortages in primary inputs). These *input multipliers* can, then, be interpreted as *forward linkages* from one sector to the rest of the economy along the value chain. In other words, it is the effect that the change in primary inputs from one industry causes in the output of all other sectors in the economy.

Nevertheless, there is a problem with the above interpretation and the concept of fixed proportions in productive factors (which is implicit in the core of the IO analysis). In Eq. 2.4, it is stated that a change in primary inputs from industry j ($\Delta \boldsymbol{v}' = [0, \ldots, \Delta v_j, \ldots, 0]$) will produce a change in the output of all other linked industries in the economy ($\Delta \boldsymbol{x} = [\Delta x1, \ldots, \Delta x_i, \ldots, \Delta x_n]$), but without a change in primary inputs of those sectors, which is in contradiction with the production function of perfect complements (or Leontief production functions).

2.2.2 *Reinterpretation as a Price Model*

To overcome the former contradiction, Dietzenbacher (1997) proposed to interpret the original Ghosh model as a *price* model instead of a *quantity* one. This, instead of $\Delta \boldsymbol{v}'$ meaning a change in quantities of primary inputs, now represents the change in value or costs of those primary inputs with the effect of changing the values of output in other sectors. Because under this interpretation the quantities remain fixed, the change in value is through changes in prices. This means that changes in the price of primary inputs will affect the price of products in other industries. This is straightforward from the fact that $x_j = p_j q_j$.

If:

$$\Delta \boldsymbol{v}_i = \boldsymbol{v}_i^{\boldsymbol{1}} - \boldsymbol{v}_i^{\boldsymbol{0}}, \tag{2.4}$$

then this leads to a change in x_j from its initial value:

$$\Delta \boldsymbol{x}_j = \boldsymbol{x}_j^{\boldsymbol{1}} - \boldsymbol{x}_j^{\boldsymbol{0}}. \tag{2.5}$$

Then, because quantities are assumed to be fixed:

$$\Delta x_j = p_j^1 q_j^0 - p_j^0 q_j^0 = \left(p_j^1 - p_j^0\right) q_j^0 = (\Delta p_j) q_j^0, \tag{2.6}$$

which clearly shows that the effect of a change in primary inputs of sector i is going to affect only the prices in the output of sector j. As can be noted, this result is the same as the one obtained in the Leontief price model, the reason for which this model can be thought of (as in the former case) as a *cost-push* input-output model.

In natural disasters (as well as in man-made ones), it has been argued that most disruptions come from the supply side of the production chain. To model the disruptions from the supply side, the concept of supply in IO analysis has been extended in the IIOM. As mentioned previously, the original IIOM was meant to be a demand-driven model. Later, Leung et al. (2007) extended the model to the supply-side price IIOM to consider the consequences of supply disruption in a disaster's aftermath. As developed earlier in this section, supply in IO analysis considers changes in prices when changes in the value added occur. This is because changes in quantities resulting from changes in value added (changes in supply side) have never been totally accepted, so the model is considered a price-change model. Nevertheless, cascade effects can be measured as the changes in final demand resulting from price changes in the supply side. The transmission mechanism is modelled through the price-demand elasticity concept, which measures the percentage change in a product's demand (in physical terms) associated with the percentage change in its price.

A further dynamic extension of the IIOM, using the supply-price model, was developed by Xu et al. (2011) in the supply-driven dynamic inoperability input-output price model (SDIIOM). On the other hand, Park (2009) used the Dietzenbacher reinterpretation of the Ghosh model as a sensitivity-price model when assessing the impacts in the US economy after Hurricanes Katrina and Rita, considering the changes in prices of the oil industry. He argued that in the short term, the inter-industry structure of the economy remained unchanged and changes in agents' behaviour to reach the equilibrium were realised through price changes. As per Leung et al.'s (2007) study, they used price elasticities to characterise changes in quantities from disruptions in prices of the oil-refinery sector.

2.2.3 Hypothetical Extraction

An additional approach to measure the importance of a sector in the economy has been created. The methodology is used to figure out what the performance of the economy would be in the counterfactual situation when sector j is missing.

As in the previous methodologies, the proportions of inputs demanded by sector j are showed in the j-th column of matrix $\boldsymbol{A}$. So, removing these (or replacing them with a column of zeros) and following the conventional way to obtain the level of production ($\boldsymbol{x}$) from final demand ($\boldsymbol{f}$), we would find the product in the hypothetical case where sector j does not demand inputs from other sectors. Let $\overline{\boldsymbol{A}}_{(cj)}$ be the technical coefficient matrix without column j; then $\overline{\boldsymbol{x}}_{(cj)} = \left(\boldsymbol{I} - \overline{\boldsymbol{A}}_{(cj)}\right)^{-1}\boldsymbol{f}$. Calculating the difference of this production level with the original one, and normalising, a measure of the backward linkages of sector j is obtained. This is:

$$\mathbf{100} * \left(x - \overline{x}_{(cj)}\right)\widehat{x}^{-1} \tag{2.7}$$

where each element of this column vector $\left(\left(x_i - \overline{x}_{(cj)i}\right)/x_j\right)$ represents the proportion on which sector i depends on sector j. The corresponding aggregated backward relevance of sector j in the economy is found to be $\boldsymbol{i}'\boldsymbol{x} - \boldsymbol{i}'\overline{\boldsymbol{x}}_{(cj)}$, which is the total change in production.

The way to find the impact of the hypothetical absence of sector j as an inter-industry supplier is analogous, but unlike *backward linkages*, this is made by subtracting the j-th row of $\boldsymbol{B}$ matrix. If $\overline{\boldsymbol{B}}_{(rj)}$ is the resulting matrix, then:

$$\overline{\boldsymbol{x}}'_{(rj)} = \boldsymbol{v}'\left(\boldsymbol{I} - \overline{\boldsymbol{B}}_{(rj)}\right)^{-1} \tag{2.8}$$

is the production vector if sector j does not supply inputs to other industries. Then, the aggregated impact from *forward linkages* in production of sector i is:

$$\boldsymbol{x}'\boldsymbol{i} - \overline{\boldsymbol{x}'}_{(rj)}\boldsymbol{i} \tag{2.9}$$

and in a disaggregated form:

$$\frac{\left(\boldsymbol{x}_i - \overline{\boldsymbol{x}}_{(rj)i}\right)}{\boldsymbol{x}_j}. \tag{2.10}$$

This stands for the dependency of sector i on purchases from sector j.

From the consideration of backward and forward linkages, a total impact of industry j in the total production of the economy can be determined. This is achieved by subtracting (or replacing by zeros) the column and row of the correspondent j-th sector in matrix $\boldsymbol{A}$ and, in this case, also the j-th value of final demand vector ($\boldsymbol{f}$). Those are expressed as $\overline{\boldsymbol{A}}_{(j)}$ and $\overline{\boldsymbol{f}}_{(j)}$, respectively. The "new" product is $\overline{\boldsymbol{x}}_{(j)}$. As in the earlier assessment of industries' relevance, the total change in the production caused by the absence of sector j accounts for its importance. This has been described as a *total linkage* measure and can be expressed in the absolute terms of changes in production: $T_j = \boldsymbol{i}'\boldsymbol{x} - \boldsymbol{i}'\overline{\boldsymbol{x}}_{(j)}$, or as percentage changes – $\overline{T}_j = 100 * \left(\boldsymbol{i}'\boldsymbol{x} - \boldsymbol{i}'\overline{\boldsymbol{x}}_{(j)}\right)/\boldsymbol{i}'\boldsymbol{x}$.

2.2.4 Applications to Disasters

Disaster impact analysis aims to account for the total impact of the shock created. As previously mentioned in this section, net linkages (or net multipliers) account for the total (direct and indirect) effects in the output from changes in input supply, or the final demand. The Regional Input-output Multiplier System (RIMS II) produces the net-output multipliers for the US economy and its subregions and considers backward linkages, having been extensively applied to disaster impact analysis. An example can be found in a study by Santos and Haimes (2004), where a reduction in the air transportation sector is simulated after the attack on the World Trade Center in 2001. According to the authors, their impact analysis showed the more vulnerable sectors through the inoperability concept as well as the possible effects on total output. Nevertheless, they recognised that backward multipliers tend to overestimate the impact due to the rigidities in the basic model.

Veen and Logtmeijer (2003) estimated the indirect impacts of major floods in the Netherlands using forward and backward linkages as a measure of flow disruptions in production after a dike breakage. They made a comparison between standard IO multipliers and ones adjusted to different scenarios. When relaxing some of the IO assumptions, mainly regarding flexibility in input and import substitutions, the estimation of the indirect effects decreased, while losses were exacerbated when considering bottlenecks in a post-disaster situation.

Recently, Xia et al. (2019) applied the hypothetical extraction method to the "Christmas" flood in York (UK) in 2015. As the IT service sector, specifically, was affected for 3 days, this method was applied to assess the impact of the knocking out of this industry on the rest of the economy. Their method was well-suited to the characteristics of the disaster, showing the economic costs of the event. The data was adjusted to the city scale and to a daily basis.

2.3 Economic-Ecological IO Model

In an ecological approach, the economic system is a subsystem that takes resources from the surrounding ecosystem, processes them for its functioning (production and consumption), and discards waste products to the ecological system (see Fig. 2.1). If the resources that the economy takes from the environment are defined as necessary commodity inputs for the production process (e.g. water, energy, land), it is possible to incorporate them into an IO analysis by adding a matrix that relates the interactions between ecological commodities usage and the industrial production process.

In the first version developed in 1968 by Herman Daly (1968), the industrial process of the model was considered under an industry-by-industry approach, while the ecological commodities included plants, animals, and even chemical reactions in the atmosphere. Nevertheless, the waste generation from the economic system to the ecological system implied the generation of a secondary commodity (the pollutant), which is in contradiction with the assumption that each industry produces only one product. To deal with this issue, Israd (1968), among others, incorporated the analysis under the commodity-by-industry approach. Since these two approaches considered the inter- and intra-relations among both the ecological and economic systems, the information requirements were of such a size that its implementation remained virtually impossible.

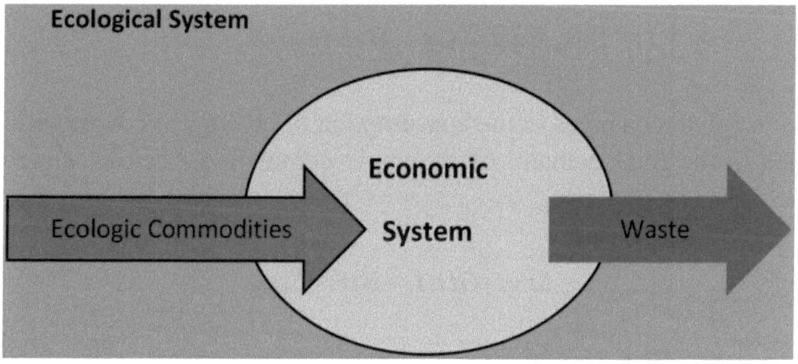

Fig. 2.1 Economic-ecological dynamics. (*Source*: based on Tukker et al. 2008)

For practical purposes, Victor (1972) considered just the ecological commodities entering the economic process and the residuals that returned into the environment. Let us start with the representation of the commodity-by-industry economic subsystem and consider that there are m commodities and n industries. Let $\boldsymbol{U} = [u_{ij}]$ be the *use* matrix where each element is the purchases of commodity i that industry j uses as their input for production. The *make* matrix $\boldsymbol{V} = [v_{ij}]$ has information about how much commodity j is produced by each sector i. The vectors for final demand and output of commodities are $\boldsymbol{e} = [e_i]$, and $\boldsymbol{x} = [x_i]$, respectively.

The next step is to define the relationships of the ecological subsystem. Let $\boldsymbol{R}$ be an array that contains the ecological commodity (i.e. CO_2, solid waste, radiation, etc.) that is deposited in the environment as a residual in the production of each economic commodity, while $\boldsymbol{T}$ is the matrix for ecological commodity use by each industry. Note that the row sums of $\boldsymbol{T}$ represent the total amount of each commodity used in the total economy production $\bar{\boldsymbol{t}} = \boldsymbol{Ti}$.

Following the standard way to obtain the proportional (or technical) coefficient matrices, each of the above is post-multiplied by $\widehat{\boldsymbol{x}}^{-1}$:

- The direct requirements of commodity-by-industry are defined as $\boldsymbol{B} = \boldsymbol{U}\widehat{\boldsymbol{x}}^{-1}$, where each element $[b_{ij}]$ represents the proportion of each commodity i needed to produce one-unit value in industry j.
- The industry-proportion matrix $\boldsymbol{C} = \boldsymbol{V}'\widehat{\boldsymbol{x}}^{-1}$ presents the proportional distribution of output from sector j for each commodity i.
- And each element $[g_{kj}]$ in matrix $\boldsymbol{G} = \boldsymbol{T}\widehat{\boldsymbol{x}}^{-1}$ represents the intensity in the use of commodity k by industry j, to produce one unit of value.
- Additionally, we can get the proportion of commodities used as inputs for production in the matrix $\boldsymbol{D} = \boldsymbol{V}'\widehat{\boldsymbol{q}}^{-1}$.

In this context, the commodity by-industry total requirement matrix is obtained with the expression $\boldsymbol{D}(\boldsymbol{I} - \boldsymbol{BD})^{-1}$. Then, $\boldsymbol{x} = \boldsymbol{D}(\boldsymbol{I} - \boldsymbol{BD})^{-1}\boldsymbol{e}$, where $\boldsymbol{e}$ is the vector for the final demand of commodities. Thus, to obtain an expression of usage for the ecological commodities in the production process, as a function of the final demand of commodities, the process is:

$$\bar{t} = Ti = [G\hat{x}]i = Gx = G\left[D(I - BD)^{-1}e\right]. \tag{2.11}$$

And as usual, the changes in the consumption of ecological commodities caused by changes in the final demand of economic commodities can be represented in differences:

$$\Delta\bar{t} = \left[GD(I - BD)^{-1}\right]\Delta e \tag{2.12}$$

where the matrix in brackets is the so-called ecological input intensity, which informs the total amount of ecological commodity k used in the production of the economic commodity i, as a result of the change in one-unit value of the final demand for that economic commodity.

Concerns about the damages in ecological services caused by disasters have arisen recently. Nevertheless, this is a topic that has not yet been deeply explored by IO modellers. One of the rare examples of this can be found in a study by Rose et al. (2000), where damages from climate change are evaluated as changes in the output of forestry-related sectors, which is an unusual application of the economic-ecological IO model. However, there exists a rising interest in evaluating the effects of disasters on ecological services, which, as Rose (2004) suggests, is a matter of environmental justice, not only in the present but in an intergenerational context to obtain sustainable results in economic systems.

2.4 Multiregional and Interregional IO

The standard IO model can evaluate the impacts in products produced from changes in final demand, but within a local economy. This is without (economic) interactions with other economies. Nevertheless, the globalised world economy establishes strong interconnections among different regions (e.g. countries), and it is increasingly evident that changes in production in one of these regions would affect other industries' production beyond local boundaries. The main channel of transmission of those effects is interregional (international) trade, by means of imports and exports.

Both the interregional IO (IRIO) and the multiregional IO (MRIO) models have been used to incorporate these relationships into IO analysis.

2.4.1 Interregional IO Model (IRIO)

The ARIO model aims to consider the inter-industry transactions among different regions, as well as the final demand of products from different regions. The information that is needed to process these relationships are the transactions between a couple of sectors (i and j) and for a p-number of regions. The transactions between a couple of regions are denoted as r and s, where $r, s = 1, 2, \ldots, p$. Information about the correspondent regional production ($\boldsymbol{x}^r$) and regional final demand ($\boldsymbol{f}^r$) is needed as well.

Let us consider that:

- $\boldsymbol{Z}^{rs}$ is the matrix of shipped inputs from region r to region s for intermediate demand. Each element of the matrix is $\left[z_{ij}^{rs}\right]$, denoting the output from industry i in region r that is needed by industry j in region s. Then, this matrix represents the intraregional transactions when $r = s$ and interregional transactions when $r \neq s$. Note that a double superscript is used only to distinguish origin and destiny region.
- $\boldsymbol{x}^r$ is the vector of total output in region r. Each element in $\boldsymbol{x}^r$, $\left[x_i^r\right]$, is the output of sector i produced in region r.
- $\boldsymbol{f}^r$ is the vector of final demand from region r. Each element in $\boldsymbol{f}^r$, $\left[f_i^r\right]$, represents the final demand of product from industry i in region r.
- The case of p regions consider the following:
- $\boldsymbol{Z} = \begin{bmatrix} & \boldsymbol{Z}^{11} \ldots \boldsymbol{Z}^{1s} \ldots \boldsymbol{Z}^{1p} & \\ \vdots & \vdots & \vdots \\ & \boldsymbol{Z}^{r1} \cdots \boldsymbol{Z}^{rs} \ldots \boldsymbol{Z}^{rp} & \\ \vdots & \vdots & \vdots \\ & \boldsymbol{Z}^{p1} \ldots \boldsymbol{Z}^{ps} \ldots \boldsymbol{Z}^{pp} & \end{bmatrix}$, where matrices in the diagonal represent intraregional transactions, while the off-diagonal matrices represent the interregional transactions. Note that while matrices in the diagonal must be squared matrices, this condition is: not necessary in the off-diagonal matrices because not all regions have the same industries. However, in the aggregate, matrix $\boldsymbol{Z}$ is a squared matrix.
- $\boldsymbol{x} = \begin{bmatrix} \boldsymbol{x}^1 \\ \vdots \\ \boldsymbol{x}^r \\ \vdots \\ \boldsymbol{x}^p \end{bmatrix}$ is the vector of total product in all regions. The dimension of the vector is $\sum_r \sum_i i^r$ (r as superscript and not as power).
- $\boldsymbol{f} = \begin{bmatrix} \boldsymbol{f}^1 \\ \vdots \\ \boldsymbol{f}^r \\ \vdots \\ \boldsymbol{f}^p \end{bmatrix}$ is the vector of final demand for all regions with dimension $\sum_r \sum_i i^r$ (r as superscript and not as power).

Once the information is arranged in a similar way as in the basic IO framework, the process to obtain the solution of the system is analogous, redefining the meaning of each coefficient.

So, once again, the system is $\boldsymbol{x} = \boldsymbol{Zi} + \boldsymbol{f}$, where each row is:

$$\begin{aligned} x_i^r - &\left[z_{i1}^{r1} + \ldots + z_{ij}^{r1} + \ldots + z_{in}^{r1}\right] + \ldots + \left[z_{i1}^{rr} + \ldots + z_{ij}^{rr} + \ldots + z_{in}^{rr}\right] \\ &+ \ldots + \left[z_{i1}^{rs} + \ldots + z_{ij}^{rs} + \ldots + z_{in}^{rs}\right] + \left[z_{i1}^{rp} + \ldots + z_{ij}^{rp} + \ldots + z_{in}^{rp}\right] \\ &+ f_i^r = \sum_s \sum_j z_{ij}^{rs} + f_i^r. \end{aligned} \tag{2.13}$$

The interregional technical coefficients are developed also in a parallel way:

Let $\boldsymbol{A}^{rs} = \boldsymbol{Z}^{rs}(\widehat{\boldsymbol{x}}^s)^{-1}$, the technical coefficients for inputs shipped by region r to region s, where each element $\left[a_{ij}^{rs} = \frac{z_{ij}^{rs}}{x_j^s}\right]$ is the proportion of input from industry i in region r that industry j in region s needs to produce one-unit value of its product (x_j^s). As before, aggregating an interregional-technical coefficients matrix, we get:

$$A = \begin{bmatrix} & A^{11} \cdots A^{1s} \ldots A^{1p} & \\ \vdots & \vdots & \vdots \\ & A^{r1} \cdots A^{rs} \ldots A^{rp} & \\ \vdots & \vdots & \vdots \\ & A^{p1} \ldots A^{ps} \ldots A^{pp} & \end{bmatrix}. \tag{2.14}$$

Using the expression in Eq. 2.13, the system can be expressed as:

$$\boldsymbol{x} = \boldsymbol{A}\boldsymbol{x} + \boldsymbol{f}. \tag{2.15}$$

And the solution is analogous to the standard model:

$$\boldsymbol{x} = (\boldsymbol{I} - \boldsymbol{A})^{-1}\boldsymbol{f} \tag{2.16}$$

where each element in $(\boldsymbol{I} - \boldsymbol{A})^{-1}$ provides information about the total change in requirements of a product of sector i in region r, **which comes not only from the change in final demand of industry *i* but also from the additional demand of inter-industrial inputs from other regions to satisfy that change in demand.**

To assess the change in final demand in region r, suppose the final demand for other sectors and regions remain constant. Then, solving the model for region r, first we can obtain an expression of other regions different from region r (where $\Delta f^s = 0$), but in terms of a product from region r:

$$(\boldsymbol{I}^{ss} - \boldsymbol{A}^{ss})\boldsymbol{x}^s - \sum_{r \neq s} \boldsymbol{A}^{sr}\boldsymbol{x}^r = \boldsymbol{0}$$

$$\boldsymbol{x}^s = (\boldsymbol{I}^{ss} - \boldsymbol{A}^{ss})^{-1}\left[\sum_{r \neq s} \boldsymbol{A}^{sr}\boldsymbol{x}^r\right] \tag{2.17}$$

The correspondent expression for region r is:

$$(\boldsymbol{I}^{rr} - \boldsymbol{A}^{rr})\boldsymbol{x}^r - \sum\nolimits_{s \neq r} \boldsymbol{A}^{rs}\boldsymbol{x}^s = \boldsymbol{f}^r \tag{2.18}$$

Substituting Eq. 2.17 in Eq. 2.18, we obtain an expression from changes in demand of region r, considering the trade effects among regions.

$$(\boldsymbol{I}^{rr} - \boldsymbol{A}^{rr})\boldsymbol{x}^r - \sum_{s \neq r} \boldsymbol{A}^{rs}\left[(\boldsymbol{I}^{ss} - \boldsymbol{A}^{ss})^{-1}\left[\sum_{r \neq s} \boldsymbol{A}^{sr}\boldsymbol{x}^r\right]\right] = \boldsymbol{f}^r. \tag{2.19}$$

In the original IO model (for one region), the production changes associated with changes in final demand were:

$$(I^{rr} - A^{rr})x^r = f^r. \tag{2.20}$$

In the interregional model, from Eq. 2.19, we realise that there is an additional term representing the demand that comes from the additional production stimulated in other regions to satisfy the original changes in final demand in region r. This is the second term in the first member of the equation:

$$\sum\nolimits_{s \neq r} A^{rs}\left[(I^{ss} - A^{ss})^{-1}\left[\sum\nolimits_{r \neq s} A^{sr}x^r\right]\right] \tag{2.21}$$

This term includes the interregional effects of changes in the final demand of one sector in one specific region on the rest of the world.

However, the high amount of data required to satisfy the IRIO model makes it virtually impossible to apply empirically.

2.4.2 *Multiregional IO (MRIO) Model*

2.4.2.1 The Basic Model

To overcome the main restriction imposed by the high data demand required by the IRIO model, various statistical techniques have been implemented to obtain a model that takes into consideration the relationships among regions but with less restrictive data requirements.

Now, the information required in the technical-regional coefficient matrix is the amount of product from industry i bought as an input in region r, to produce one-value unit of industry j's product in region r, denoted as z^r (note that only the region of destiny is referred to in the superscript). This means that information on the product's origin is not necessary in this model and the technical coefficients can be found following a method similar to a standard IO model: $a_{ij}^r = \frac{z_{ij}^r}{x_j^r}$. The meaning of these coefficients is the proportion of a product from industry i used as input by industry j in region r to produce one-unit value of output in industry j in region r (x_j^r). The common way to obtain this information is through scaling from the national technical coefficients to a regional technical coefficient matrix, weighted by the proportional product of each destiny subindustry in the total production of a destiny industry. Assuming that a_{ij}^n is the proportion of input from sector i needed in industry j to produce one-unit value of x_j in the entire multiregional chain, and assuming that industry j posses h subindustries in region r, then the weighted regional-technical coefficients can be found as follows:

$$a_{ij}^{r} = \frac{\sum_{h} a_{i(j,h)}^{n} x_{i(j,h)}^{r}}{x_{j}^{r}} \tag{2.22}$$

where $x_j^r = \sum_h x_{i(j,h)}^r$. These are the elements of matrix $\boldsymbol{A}^r$ which are parallel to $\boldsymbol{A}^{rr}$ in the IRIO model when $r = s$, i.e. the elements of the diagonal in matrix $\boldsymbol{A}$ represent intraregional transactions.

For interregional coefficients, the information is compiled in a different way due to the usual available data. The interregional table for industry i's product contains the amount of input i, from region r to region s ($\boldsymbol{Z}_i = \left[z_i^{rs}\right]$), regardless of the destination industry. The column sum of the s-th region contains the total amount that a region bought of good i from all other regions ($T_i^s = \sum_r z_i^{rs}$). Dividing each element of $\boldsymbol{Z}_i$ between its correspondent column sum, the input i that comes from region r as a proportion of all input i shipped in region s: $c_i^{rs} = \frac{z_i^{rs}}{T_i^s}$ is obtained.

Let $c^{rs} = \begin{bmatrix} c_1^{rs} \\ \vdots \\ c_n^{rs} \end{bmatrix}$ be a vector array that contains only one specific origin-destination for each industrial good, where intraregional transactions arise as the case $r = s$.

With all these elements, we can construct the MRIO in an equivalent way with the IRIO model. The counterpart in the MRIO model for matrix $\boldsymbol{A}^{rs}$ in the IRIO model is now:

$$\widehat{c}^{rs} A^{r} = \begin{bmatrix} c_1^{rs} a_{11}^{r} & \cdots & c_1^{rs} a_{1n}^{r} \\ \vdots & c_i^{rs} a_{ij}^{r} & \vdots \\ c_n^{rs} a_{n1}^{r} & \cdots & c_n^{rs} a_{nn}^{r} \end{bmatrix} \tag{2.23}$$

Then, the MRIO model is:

$$\begin{aligned} \boldsymbol{x} &= \boldsymbol{CAx} + \boldsymbol{Cf} \\ (\boldsymbol{I} - \boldsymbol{CA})\boldsymbol{x} &= \boldsymbol{Cf}. \end{aligned} \tag{2.24}$$

Note that in this case, the proportion of products from region r used to satisfy the total final demand in other regions is explicit. Thus, the solution to obtain the product as a function of the final demand of the system is:

$$\boldsymbol{x} = (\boldsymbol{I} - \boldsymbol{CA})^{-1}\boldsymbol{Cf}. \tag{2.25}$$

Similarly, as in the IRIO model, an extended expression of the model is as follows:

$$\begin{aligned} &(\boldsymbol{I}^s - \widehat{\boldsymbol{c}}^{sr}\boldsymbol{A}^s)\boldsymbol{x}^s - \sum_{r \neq s} \widehat{\boldsymbol{c}}^{sr}\boldsymbol{A}^r\boldsymbol{x}^r = \boldsymbol{0} \\ &\boldsymbol{x}^s = (\boldsymbol{I}^s - \widehat{\boldsymbol{c}}^{sr}\boldsymbol{A}^s)^{-1}\left[\sum\nolimits_{r \neq s} \widehat{\boldsymbol{c}}^{sr}\boldsymbol{A}^r\boldsymbol{x}^r\right]. \end{aligned} \tag{2.26}$$

The correspondent expression for region r is:

$$(\boldsymbol{I}^r - \widehat{\boldsymbol{c}}^{rr}\boldsymbol{A}^r)\,\boldsymbol{x}^r - \sum_{s \neq r} \widehat{\boldsymbol{c}}^{rs}\boldsymbol{A}^s\boldsymbol{x}^s = \sum_r \widehat{\boldsymbol{c}}^{sr}\boldsymbol{f}^r. \tag{2.27}$$

Substituting Eq. 2.26 into Eq. 2.27, an expression is obtained that solves for the product in region r, from changes in demand of region r, taking into consideration the trade effects among regions:

$$(I^r - \widehat{c}^{rr}A^r)x^r - \sum_{s \neq r} \widehat{c}^{rs}A^s \left[(I^s - \widehat{c}^{sr}A^s)^{-1} \left[\sum_{r \neq s} \widehat{c}^{sr}A^r x^r \right] \right] = \sum_r \widehat{c}^{sr}f^r. \tag{2.28}$$

Because we had stated the similarity between $\boldsymbol{A}^{rr}$ and $(\widehat{\boldsymbol{c}}^{rr}\boldsymbol{A}^r)$, as expressed in the IRIO model, the term $(\boldsymbol{I}^r - \widehat{\boldsymbol{c}}^{rr}\boldsymbol{A}^r)$ in Eq. 2.28 associated with levels of $\boldsymbol{x}^r$ represents the impact related to changes in final demand in the regional economy, but without considering the multiregional effects associated with trade. The additional term, $\sum_{s \neq r} \widehat{\boldsymbol{c}}^{rs}\boldsymbol{A}^s \left[(\boldsymbol{I}^s - \widehat{\boldsymbol{c}}^{sr}\boldsymbol{A}^s)^{-1} \left[\sum_{r \neq s} \widehat{\boldsymbol{c}}^{sr}\boldsymbol{A}^r\boldsymbol{x}^r \right] \right]$, refers to this interregional feedback caused by changes in demand in other regions of the suppliers of the region where the first impulse of final demand originated. It is important to note that unlike the IRIO model, the impacts in region r's output in the above expression account for final demand changes in all regions, weighted by the share of that demand that is fulfilled from region r. Instead of seeing the left term in Eq. 2.28 as the impact from changes in final demand of a certain region (as usually happens in the IO framework), it is the impact in output of a certain region from changes in the demand of its products from all other regions.

2.4.2.2 Applications to Disasters

With strong interregional economic relationships, changes in one region can affect others. As a result, multiregional analysis has become a necessity in disaster impact analysis. The most common regional model used is the MRIO, which contains data about inputs bought by sector i in region r from sector j (it does not matter where the inputs come from); and even when this data is not available, the technical coefficients can be calculated using the product mix approach (Miller and Blair 2009). This has made the assessment of higher-order costs possible in the context of a disaster affecting small regions rather than national economies and its dispersed effects in multiple regions (Haimes et al. 2005; Okuyama 2004). For instance, Crowther and Haimes (2010) go beyond the IIOM to make the multiregional dimension explicit in their multiregional inoperability IO model (MIIOM). They deal specifically with the lack of spatial explicitness in earlier models. This makes the model more accurate at a regional level (or even down to the county level), where in the past the impacts and damages were considered homogenous or uniform across the region. The conclusion is that it benefits providences for better preparedness at a multiregional level. The MIIOM allows the consideration of the relationships between different regions. In its initial version, it was a demand-driven model; however, the authors argue that inoperability is more an issue of lost supply value, which resulted in an extension of the MIIOM to take into consideration the inoperability in production from bottlenecks in production (supply chain). One of the limitations of the model is that the dynamic aspect of recovery is not modelled.

All these reviewed versions of IO analysis represent the bases for most of the IO modelling used to assess the economic impact of disasters. They are considered, especially the last one, the multiregional IO model, as the basis for the Multiregional Flood Footprint model.

2.5 IO Approach for Disaster Impact Analysis: Indirect Cost Appraisal

As said at the beginning of the previous section, the original version of the IO model is static and demand driven. Nevertheless, the damage caused by a disaster imposes imbalances in the economy that usually affects the supply side of the productive chain, leading to bottlenecks in production and disrupting the economic equilibrium during recovery. In this section, further research will be presented on the specific situations that arise after a disaster and the way they have been incorporated under the framework of IO analysis.

2.5.1 *Modelling the Risks*

The occurrence and intensity of disasters are often difficult to predict with any level of certainty. Leveraging the structure of IO analysis and the data available, some extensions have been made to explicitly incorporate inherent risk from disasters. Several authors (Haimes and Jiang 2001; Haimes et al. 2005; Santos 2006) have developed a measure of expected inoperability based on the risk of the system to becoming unable to perform its planned *natural or engineered functions*. Based on this concept, the IIOM assumes a direct relationship between the number of transactions and the interdependency between economic industries.

The matrix of technical coefficients ($\boldsymbol{A}$) turns into a matrix where the coefficients represent the strength of the relationship between sectors, ($\boldsymbol{A}^*$), where every element $[a_{ij}^*]$ represents the inoperability in industry i attributable to industry j. In its initial version, this is a demand-driven and static model where equilibrium is assumed at each period during the recovery process (Santos and Haimes 2004). Even with its rigidities, the IIOM has been proven useful in the assessment of inoperability among industries to prepare for, or mitigate against, the adverse impacts of negative shocks when identifying sectors that are the most vulnerable to them (Crowther et al. 2007).

2.5.2 Time-Dynamic Extensions

As mentioned before, a disaster leaves its footprint in the economy for a certain period, depending on the characteristics of the disaster (mainly, duration and intensity). For instance, an earthquake may last only few seconds while its consequences can be felt for a long time afterwards. On the other hand, the consequences of a flood that lasts for some weeks can be less harmful if infrastructure is not seriously damaged (Okuyama 2009). One of the principal challenges is to understand the process by which an economy recovers, since this largely determines the indirect costs and, therefore, the total costs. Even though the standard IO model is static, Leontief, himself, developed a dynamic extension (Miller and Blair 2009; Rose 1995). Later extensions developed to deal with these constraints are the sequential inter-industry model (SIM) (Okuyama 2004; Romanoff and Levine 1981), a continuous-time formulation of the regional econometric IO model (REIOM) and the dynamic inoperability IO model (DIIOM) (Haimes et al. 2005; Okuyama 2007; Santos and Rehman 2012; Santos 2006; Xu et al. 2011). Other important developments in this field were made by Hallegatte (2008), who uses a time-scaled approach to model the recovery path, in which supply constraints and bottlenecks are also considered.

2.5.3 Modelling Imbalances

The basic IO model and some of its mentioned extensions are used in a situation where the economy is in equilibrium and production is totally consumed by intermediate and final demand, even in a disaster aftermath. However, the damage caused by disasters usually leads to a structural disruption in the normal functioning of the economy. The production capacity is reduced and imbalances between supply and demand arise.

In practice, it is noticeable that these imbalances usually remain until the economy completely recovers (Li et al. 2013; Okuyama 2009). To deal with the consequences of damaged production capacity, bottlenecks, and imbalances, in general, important adjustments to the IO model have been made. With this purpose, the notion of the basic equation was developed as a modification of the IO closed model (Bockarjova et al. 2004; Steenge and Bočkarjova 2007), as the starting point of the economy before a disaster, and as a path towards its pre-equilibrium state.

A further development from the basic equation was the impact modelling of a disaster using an event account matrix (EAM). This is an IO-compatible element used to assess the impact of a disaster (or a shortage in productive capacity, in general) on the economic system (Cole 2003; Hallegatte 2008; Li et al. 2013; Steenge and Bočkarjova 2007). The aim is to generate a matrix with the proportion of damage to each sector, which allows an estimation of the imbalances between the productive capacity and consumption in an economy after a shock. After this post-disaster starting point, a recovery strategy simulation is conducted.

The modelling of the recovery process allows for the substitution of imports for some goods and services and deals with constrains in production and bottlenecks that arise after the disaster. The effectiveness of the strategy and recovery path largely depends on the reallocation criteria of the remaining productive factors (Batey and Rose 1990; Ghosh 1958; Hallegatte 2008; Hallegatte and Przyluski 2010; Li et al. 2013).

Other treatments of changes in supply are developing as extensions of the IIOM. For instance, Leung et al. (2007) use a price-changing approach to try to overcome the main limitations of demand-driven IO analysis.

For example, Xu et al. (2011) developed an extension of the classical inoperability IO model. The extension is a supply-driven model, which makes it more suitable for a situation where there are imbalances (disequilibrium between production and demand), and they developed it in the frame of earlier dynamic models. Their model, the DIIOM, accounts for a recovery path through time. The first modification is based on the IIOM, which is not dynamic but is driven by changes in value-added instead of changes in final demand. Even if this price model only captures the changes in the prices of the value added (labour, taxes, etc.), it can be suitable to analyse the recovery path of economic sectors after a disaster. What is not explicit in the model is if it is comparable with a demand-driven model, because the impact in the economy caused by a disaster is modelled as an increase in the level of prices of industries' products. One of the weaknesses of this model is the fact that the recovery time for each affected sector is assumed. This is usually one of the expected results from the analysis, instead of an input. However, Santos and Rehman (2012) extended the model and made their analysis based on survey data to calibrate or estimate the time for recovery in the affected sectors.

In further extensions, Li et al. (2013) developed a dynamic inequalities approach, an IO-based model which presents "a theoretical route map for imbalanced economic recovery." The main achievement of their model is the consideration of supply constraints (using the EAM concept) and changes in final demand. They also consider the imbalances in the economy during the recovery time process. In this sense, it is a time-dynamic model. Substitution in imports is also allowed for the *recovery* demand.

2.5.4 Recent Developments

Three relevant extensions for impact assessment have been developed in recent years: (a) the incorporation of hypothetical extractions, (b) the use of Cobb-Douglas functions, and (c) the adoption of nonlinear programming.

Dietzenbacher and Lahr (2013) apply the method of hypothetical extractions to the analysis of impact analysis. This method proposes to *extract*, partially or totally, the intermediate transactions of a sector within the economy. It achieves this by replacing the row and column of the affected sector with zeros (or smaller proportions of the original value). A new level of production is calculated under these conditions. The change from the original level of production constitutes the effect of the disaster in the economy. The main contribution of this approach is that it consistently considers the forward effects of a shock within the demand-driven IO model. However, Oosterhaven and Bouwmeester (2016) have argued that the assessment of forward effects with this method is flawed, arguing that what is measured are the backward effects of the reduction of intermediate sales of an industry, not the forward effects of the reduction of inputs from the affected industry to the other purchasing industries.

Koks et al. (2014) proposed to use a Cobb-Douglas function to estimate the direct costs from labour and capital constraints, and the indirect costs incurred during the recovery process are derived through the adaptive regional input-output (ARIO) model (Hallegatte 2008). This approach provides consistency within the economic theory to the appraisal of effects in a flow variable (the production) that arise from damages in a stock variable (capital stock). It should be noted that the consideration of the relationship between the productive factors and production levels through the Cobb-Douglas function is to convert the physical damages to capital stock into shortages in the production flow.

More recently, Oosterhaven and Bouwmeester (2016) proposed a new approach, which is based on a nonlinear programming model that minimises the information gain between the pre-disaster and post-disaster situation of economic transactions. This model is successful in reproducing the recovery towards the pre-disaster economic equilibrium. The model has been tested hypothetically, and further development is required before applying it to real cases.

Related to this approach, Koks and Thissen (2016) developed a dynamic optimisation model based on a linear programming model and IO supply-use tables, the multiregional impact assessment model (MRIA), which accounts for supply constraints as the appraisal of production losses in the impacted region, the production required to overcome the former losses, and the production required in a broader region to satisfy demand for reconstruction. The hypothetical results for a flood in Rotterdam show that the ratio of indirect/direct losses increases with the intensity of the event, which may be the result of some flexibilities regarding the substitution possibilities in the MRIA.

Further, Oosterhaven and Többen (2017) applied this approach with a multiregional supply-use table (MRSUT) to overcome the limitations of fixed industry market shares. They developed a nonlinear programming model and applied it to the heavy flooding in Germany in 2013.

Based on the literature review, the IO analysis strengths lie in its ability to incorporate various situations arising in the economy after a disaster, and owing to this, it serves as the basis of the theoretical and analytical framework for the analysis used in this book. The developed approach is particularly focused by Li et al. (2013).

Chapter 3
The Flood Footprint Analysis: A Proposal

The rationale of the standard *flood footprint analysis* (FFA) is disclosed in detail in this chapter. This analysis is proposed to comprehensively include both direct and indirect costs arising from a disaster.

It is worth noting that this model gets its name from a specific type of disaster: flooding events, mainly because of the characteristics of this type of disaster and the context within which the research originated – a region heavily affected by floods. However, the model is flexible enough to be applied to other types of extreme climate events. So, for modelling purposes, hereinafter the term flood is used interchangeably with natural disaster.

Firstly, we introduce the basic version of the FFA and expand it to a multiregional version in the following section, the *multiregional* flood footprint analysis (MFFA).

3.1 Flood Footprint for a Single Region

Let us start with IO considerations. The IO model is founded on the basic idea of the circular flow of an economy in equilibrium. The IO tables present the inter-industrial transactions of the whole economy in a linear array. In mathematical notation this is presented as:

$$x = Ax + f \tag{3.1}$$

where x is a vector representing the total production of each industrial sector;[1] Ax represents the intermediate demand vector where each element of the matrix A, $[a_{ij}]$

The development of the single-region FFM is derived from Mendoza-Tinoco et al. (2017).

[1] In the modelling, it is assumed that each industry produces only one uniform product.

© The Author(s), under exclusive license to Springer Nature Switzerland AG 2023

D. Mendoza-Tinoco et al., *Multiregional Flood Footprint Analysis*, SpringerBriefs in Economics, https://doi.org/10.1007/978-3-031-29728-1_3

refers to the technology, showing product i, which is needed to produce one unit of product j; and f indicates the final demand vector of products from each industry.

Based on the IO analysis, the cost appraisal in the *flood footprint modelling* departs from the *basic equation*, a concept developed by Steenge and Bočkarjova (2007). This is a closed[2] IO model that represents an economy in equilibrium. Equilibrium implies that total production equals total demand with full employment of productive factors, including both capital and labour, as in Eq. 3.2:

$$\begin{bmatrix} A & f/l \\ l' & 0 \end{bmatrix} \begin{pmatrix} x \\ l \end{pmatrix} = \begin{pmatrix} x \\ l \end{pmatrix} \tag{3.2}$$

and

$$l = l'x \tag{3.3}$$

where l' is a row vector of *technical labour* coefficients for each industry, showing the relation of labour needed in each industry to produce one unit of product: $\left[\frac{L_i}{x_i}\right]$. L_i is the industrial level of employment. The scalar l is the total level of employment in the economy.

All inter-industrial flows of products, as well as industrial employment, are considered as necessary inputs involved in the production of each unit of output. A linear relationship between the productive factors (labour and capital) and the output in each sector is assumed in the IO analysis, suggesting that inputs should be invested in fixed proportions for proportional expansion in output.

However, experience has demonstrated that the economy equilibrium is broken after a disaster, and inequalities arise between productive capacity and demand. In the next section, we introduce the possible sources of these inequalities.

3.1.1 Sources of Post-disaster Inequalities

After a disaster, market forces become imbalanced, leading to gaps between supply and demand in different markets. The causes of these imbalances may be varied, and they constitute the origin of the ripple effects that permeate in the whole economic system.

---

[2] Here, *closed* means that the primary productive factors (labour) are explicitly considered within the model.

3.1.1.1 Labour Productivity Constraints

The production functions in the IO model assume a complement-type technology where the productive factors (labour and capital) maintain fixed proportions in the production process. Constraints in any of the productive factors will produce, therefore, a proportional decline in productive capacity, even when other factors remain fully available. Therefore, labour constraints after a disaster may impose severe knock-on effects on the rest of the economy. This is particularly true in the short run after a disaster, when supplier substitution is difficult and there are not many options to rearrange production processes. This situation makes labour constraints a key factor to consider in disaster impact analysis. In the *flood footprint* model, these constraints can arise from the employees' inability to work because of illness or death or from commuting delays due to damaged or malfunctioning transportation infrastructure. In the model, the proportion of surviving production capacity from the constrained labour productive capacity (x_l^t) after the shock is:

$$x_l^t = \left(i - \Gamma_l^t\right). * x^0 \tag{3.4}$$

and

$$\Gamma_l^t = \left(l^0 - l^t\right)./l^0 \tag{3.5}$$

where Γ_l^t is the event account vector (EAV) for labour, following Steenge and Bočkarjova (2007), where each element contains the proportion of labour that is unavailable at each time t after the flooding. l^0 and l^t represent the pre-disaster vector and the *t-th* period of industrial labour, respectively. Vector i is a vector of ones of the same dimension as Γ_l^t, so the vector $\left(i - \Gamma_l^t\right)$ contains the surviving proportion of employment at time t. x^0 is the pre-disaster level of production.

The proportion of the surviving productive capacity of labour is, thus, a function of the loss from the industrial labour force and its pre-disaster employment level. Following the fixed proportion assumption of the production functions, the productive capacity of labour after the disaster (x_l^t) will be a linear proportion of the surviving labour capacity at each period.

3.1.1.2 Capital Productivity Constraints

Similar to labour constraints, the flooding aftermath (x_{cap}^t), productive capacity from industrial capital will be constrained by the surviving capacity of the industrial capital. The share of damage to each industry is disclosed in the event account vector (EAV) for capital. Then, the remaining production capacity of industrial capital at each time step, is:

$$x_{\text{cap}}^t = \left(I - \Gamma_{\text{cap}}^t\right) * x^0 \tag{3.6}$$

and

$$\Gamma_{\text{cap}}^{t} = \left(k^{0} - k^{t}\right)./k^{0} \tag{3.7}$$

where, x^0 is the pre-disaster level of production and Γ_{cap}^{t} is the EAV, a column vector showing the share of damages of productive capital in each industry. k_0 is the vector of capital stock in each industry in the pre-disaster situation, and k^t is the surviving capital stock in each industry at time t during the recovery process.

During the recovery, the productive capacity of industrial capital is restored gradually through local production for both reconstruction and imports.

3.1.1.3 Post-disaster Final Demand

Final demand may vary for diverse reasons. On the one hand, the recovery process involves the reconstruction and replacement of damaged physical capital, which increases the final demand for those sectors involved in the reconstruction process, namely, the *reconstruction demand,* f_{rec}. On the other hand, final demand may also decrease after a disaster. Li et al. (2013) have noted that after a disaster, strategic adaptive behaviour would lead people to ensure their continued consumption of basic commodities, such as food and medical services, while reducing consumption of other non-basic products.

In this model, we consider the adaptive consumption behaviour of households. Here, the demand for non-basic goods is assumed to decline immediately after the disaster, while consumption in industries providing food, energy, clothing, and medical services remains at pre-disaster levels.

Recovery in household consumption is driven by two complementary processes. For consumption adaptation, we consider a short-run tendency parameter (d_1^t), which is modelled as the rate of recovery in consumption in each period. The rationale here is that consumers restore their consumption according to market signals about the recovery process. Likewise, a long-run tendency parameter (d_2^t) is calculated as a *recovery gap,* i.e. the total demand minus the total production capacity compared against the total demand in each period. Therefore, the expression for dynamic household consumption recovery is:

$$f_{hh}^{t} = \left(\mu^{0} + d_1^t + d_2^t\right). * c^{0} \tag{3.8}$$

where the parameter μ^0 expresses the reduced proportion of household demand (a parameter similar to the EAV) over time, and vector c^0 represents the pre-disaster level of household expenditures on products by industry.

The rest of the final demand categories recover proportionally to the economy, based on the contribution of each category to the pre-disaster final demand. It is essential to note that a tradeoff exists between the resources allocated to final demand and to reconstruction purposes, as the inequalities between supply and demand will remain, at least until reconstruction is completed. The adapted total final demand (f^t), then, is modelled as follows:

$$f^t = \sum_k f_k^t + f_{\text{rec}}^t \tag{3.9}$$

where f^t is the adapted total final demand at time t, including the reconstruction demand for damaged industrial and residential capital ($f_{\text{rec}}^t = f_{\text{cap}}^t + f_{hh}^t$). It also includes the final demand for all final consumption categories, indicated by the summation $\sum_k f_k^t$, where the subscript k refers to the vector of each category of final consumption. $k = 1$ is the adapted household consumption (f_{hh}^t), $k = 2$ is government expenditure, $k = 3$ is investment in capital formation, and $k = 4$ is external consumption or exports.

The adapted total demand for each sector, (x_{td}^t), can thus be interpreted as follows:

$$x_{td}^t(i) = \sum_{j=1}^{n} a_{ij} x_{td}^t(j) + f^t(i). \tag{3.10}$$

Equations 3.4, 3.5, 3.6, 3.7, 3.8, 3.9 and 3.10 describe the changes on both sides of the economy's flow (production and consumption) where imbalances in the economy after a disaster arise from the differences in the productive capacity of labour, the productive capacity of industrial capital, and changes in final demand. From this point, the restoration process starts to return the economy to its pre-disaster equilibrium production level.

3.1.2 Post-disaster Recovery Process

The following section describes the process of recovery. Here, an economy can be considered as recovered once its labour and industrial production capacities are in equilibrium with total demand and its production is restored to its pre-disaster level. How to use the remaining resources to achieve pre-disaster conditions is modelled based on a selected rationing scheme.

The first step is to determine the available production capacity in each period after the disaster. Within the context of Leontief production functions, the productive capacity is determined for the minimum of both productive factors, capital, or labour, as shown below:

$$x_{tp}^t = \min\left\{x_{\text{cap}}^t, x_l^t\right\}. \tag{3.11}$$

Secondly, the level of the constrained production capacity is compared with the adapted total demand to determine the allocation strategy for the remaining resources and for reconstruction planning. The rules of this process constitute what it is called the *rationing scheme*, described below.

3.1.2.1 Rationing Scheme

The recovery process requires allocating the remaining resources to satisfy society's needs during a disaster's aftermath. Thus, the question of how to distribute and prioritise the available production based on the remaining capacity of industry or final customer demand becomes essential, as recovery time and indirect costs can vary widely under different rationing schemes.

In this research, we used a *proportional prioritisation* rationing scheme that first allocates the remaining production among the inter-industrial demand (Ax^t_{tp}) and then attends to the categories of final demand.[3] This assumption is built on the rationale that business-to-business transactions are prioritised, based on the observation that these relationships are stronger than business-to-client relationships (Hallegatte 2008; Li et al. 2013). However, the model is flexible enough to test diverse *rationing schemes*.

Thus, when calculating the productive possibilities of the next period, the actual production is first compared with inter-industrial demand. If $O^t(i) = \sum_j A(i,j)x^t_{tp}(j)$ is the production required in industry i to satisfy the intermediate demand of all other industries, two possible scenarios may arise after the disaster (Hallegatte 2008):

The first scenario occurs when $x^t_{tp}(i) < O^t(i)$, in which case the production from industry i at time t in the post-disaster situation ($x^t_{tp}(i)$) cannot satisfy the intermediate demands of other industries. This situation constitutes a bottleneck in the production chain, where production in industry j is then constrained by $\frac{x^t_{tp}(i)}{O^t(i)}x^t_{tp}(j)$, where $\frac{x^t_{tp}(i)}{O^t(i)}$ is the proportion restricting the production in industry j, $x^t_{tp}(j)$. This process proceeds for each industry, after which there must be consideration of the fact that industries producing less will also demand less, affecting and reducing, in turn, the production of other industries. The iteration of this process continues until production capacity can satisfy this *adapted* intermediate demand, and in the process, the remaining production is canalised to satisfy part of the final and *reconstruction* demands to increase the productive capacity during the next period. This situation leads to a partial equilibrium, where the level of the adapted intermediate demand is defined as $Ax^{t^*}_{tp}$ and where the asterisk in $x^{t^*}_{tp}$ represents the adapted production capacity that provides the partial equilibrium and is not bigger than the actual production capacity (x^t_{tp}) from Eq. (3.11).[4]

This process continues until the total production available at each time, $x^t_{tp}(i)$, can satisfy the intermediate demand at time t, O^t.

[3]We assume here that the productivity of any of the productive factors does not change during the recovery process, as is the case with Leontief production functions. We also assume that the disaster happens just after time $t = 0$ and that the recovery process starts at time $t = 1$.

[4]Adapted production capacity, $x^{t^*}_{tp}$, and actual production capacity, x^t_{tp}, are equal just in the case all sectors can satisfy their respective intermediate demand. Otherwise, $x^{t^*}_{tp}$, is still smaller than x^t_{tp}.

The second scenario occurs when $x_{tp}^{t}(i) > O^{t}(i)$. Then, the intermediate demand can be satisfied without affecting the production of other industries, although final demand may not be fully satisfied.

In both cases, the remaining production after satisfying the intermediate demand is proportionally allocated to the recovery demand and to other final demand categories in accordance with the following expressions:

$$\left(x_{tp}^{t} - Ax_{tp}^{t}\right) .* f_{k}^{0} ./ \left(\sum_{k} f_{k}^{0} + f_{\mathrm{rec}}^{t}\right) \tag{3.12}$$

$$\left(x_{tp}^{t} - Ax_{tp}^{t}\right) .* f_{\mathrm{rec}}^{t} ./ \left(\sum_{k} f_{k}^{0} + f_{\mathrm{rec}}^{t}\right). \tag{3.13}$$

Equation 3.12 refers to the distribution of product to the k categories of final demand, while Eq. 3.13 refers to the proportion of available product that is designated to reconstruction.

The expression $\left(x_{tp}^{t} - Ax_{tp}^{t}\right)$ refers to the production left after satisfying the intermediate demand, and $\sum_{k} f_{k}^{0}$ refers to the total final demand in the pre-disaster period such that the production left after satisfying intermediate demand is allocated among the categories of final demand following the proportions of the pre-disaster condition plus the consideration of the reconstruction needs for recovery (f_{rec}^{t}). Note that for the first scenario, the expression Ax_{tp}^{t} represents the *adapted intermediate demand* ($x_{tp}^{t^*}$), which is smaller than the actual production capacity, x_{tp}^{t}.

There is another element involved in reconstruction efforts that is considered in the model. We assume that part of the unsatisfied final demand is covered by imports, some of which contribute to the recovery when allocated to *reconstruction demand*.

3.1.2.2 Imports

In the *flood footprint* model, imports help in the reconstruction process by supplying some of the inputs that are not internally available to meet *reconstruction* demand. Additionally, if the damaged production capacity is not able to satisfy the demand of final consumers, they will rely on imports until internal production is restored and they can return to their previous suppliers.

There are some assumptions underlying imports. First, imports will be allocated proportionally among final demand categories and reconstruction demand. Second, commodities from other regions are assumed to be always available for provision at the maximum rate of import under the pre-disaster condition. Third, there are some types of goods and services that, by nature, are usually supplied locally (such as utilities and transport services), so, in the short term, it is not feasible for them to be acquired through imports. Finally, imports are assumed to be constrained by the total *importability capacity*, which here is defined as the survival productive capacity of the transport sectors (see Eq. 3.14). The assumption is that the capacity of transporting goods is proportional to the productive capacity of the sectors related to transport, so that if the production value of sectors related to transport services is contracted by $x\%$ in time t, the imports will be contracted in the same proportion with reference to the pre-disaster level of imports, m^t:

$$m^t = \left(\frac{x_{\text{tran}}^{*(t)}}{x_{\text{tran}}^{0}} * m^0 \right) \tag{3.14}$$

where m^0 is the vector of pre-disaster imports and x_{tran}^{0} and $x_{\text{tran}}^{*(t)}$ are the scalars denoting the pre-disaster and post-disaster production capacities of the sectors related to transport. The subscript tran refers to aggregated transport sectors by land, water, and air. If two or more sectors are related to transport, then x_{tran}^{0} is the sum of the production in those sectors at the pre-disaster level, and $x_{\text{tran}}^{*(t)}$ is the production in those sectors at time t during recovery obtained from the vectors of productive capacity, x^0 and $x^{*(t)}$, respectively.

3.1.2.3 Recovery Process

Decisions to return to pre-disaster conditions can be complex and varied. Here, we have assumed a way of adapting to a condition of balanced production and demand. That is to say, we pursue a partial equilibrium for productive capacities at each time (through the rationing scheme) and then follow a long-term growth tendency towards the pre-disaster level of production (through the reconstruction efforts).

It should be remembered that the recovery process includes the repair and/or replacement of damaged capital stock and households. During this process, production capacity increases, both through local production and through imports allocated to *reconstruction demand.*

Then, the productive capacity of each industry for the next period incorporates the rebuilt capacity of the last period:

$$x_{\text{cap}}^{t+1}(i) = x_{\text{cap}}^{t}(i) + g\left\{ \left[m^t(i) + \left(x_{tp}^{t}(i) - \sum_{j=1}^{n} a_{ij} x_{tp}^{t}(j) \right) \right] * \left[f_{\text{cap}}^{t}(i)./\left(\sum f_k^0 + f_{\text{rec}}^{t} \right) \right] \right\} \tag{3.15}$$

where g is the generic function that includes the relation of capital production recovery.

Note that the proportion of affected capital (the EAV) changes for each industry as follows:

$$\gamma_i^{t+1} - \gamma_i^t = \frac{\{[m^t(i) + (x_{tp}^t(i) - \sum_{j=1}^{n} a_{ij} x_{tp}^t(j))] * [f_{\text{cap}}^t(i)./(\sum f_k^0 + f_{\text{rec}}^t)]\}}{f_{\text{rec}}^0} \quad (3.16)$$

This new level of production is compared with the level of labour capacity at the next period. The actual production level in each period is the minimum of both. Then, the process described above is repeated until an equilibrated economy at the pre-disaster production level is reached.

The driving forces of recovery are constituted, then, by the progressive restoration of the productive capacity of industrial capital by means of internal production and imports allocated to *reconstruction* demand, by the restoration of the labour force, and by the recovery of final demand.

3.1.3 Flood Footprint Modelling Outcomes

3.1.3.1 Direct and Indirect Costs

The flood footprint model provides outcome results for a variety of economic variables over the course of the recovery process. All results are provided at each period during restoration and at a disaggregation level of industrial sectors available in the IO tables. The time that each variable and sector require to achieve its pre-disaster level is, likewise, provided by the model. Results of *direct* and *indirect costs* constitute the principal outcomes of the model.

The *direct costs* account for the value and the proportion of damages to the physical infrastructure, both to industrial and residential capital. To determine these, we construct the EAV with the damage proportional to the capital stock at the reconstruction cost. The model, in turn, translates the damage from this *stock variable* into damages to productivity, a *flow variable*, through the production functions.

The *indirect costs* account, period by period, for the non-realised production owing to the existence of constraints in both productivity and demand, i.e. effects cascading from the *direct costs*.

The model delivers dynamics of recovery for other variables, as well, such as the restoration in industrial productive capacity, labour productive capacity, the contribution of imports to the economy during the recovery process, and final demand dynamics of the restoration of levels of consumption in each category.

It should be noted that the recovery trajectories of the variables are influenced by the assumptions and decisions considered for reconstruction, such as the *rationing scheme* configuration. On the other hand, a sensitivity analysis of parameters is performed for robustness of results and to determine how sensitive the results are to changes in the parameters.

3.1.3.2 Flowchart for Flood Footprint Modelling

Figure 3.1 summarises the workflow (modelling process) for estimating the total cumulative economic impact of a flooding event, or the *flood footprint*. It should be remembered that this analysis is applicable to other disasters, as well. The entire process can be summarised in six steps. The aim of recovery is to return to the equilibrium and to return to the production level of the pre-disaster condition.

Step 1 Obtain exogenous inputs for the flood footprint model. The white boxes in Fig. 3.1 detail the input data and factors required.

- Natural hazard severity and characteristics of the disaster (top-left white boxes) define the studied event when employing this model's framework. This can potentially also link with global/regional climatic change scenarios to model precipitation levels, etc. for future hazards (e.g. 1/100 year's flooding or 1/1000 year's flooding event).
- Investment/capital matrix and policy intervention recovery (top-middle white boxes) describe external factors that will be influencing recovery patterns, for example, governmental activities including extra investment for reconstruction. The capital matrix determines investments needed to restore production capacity

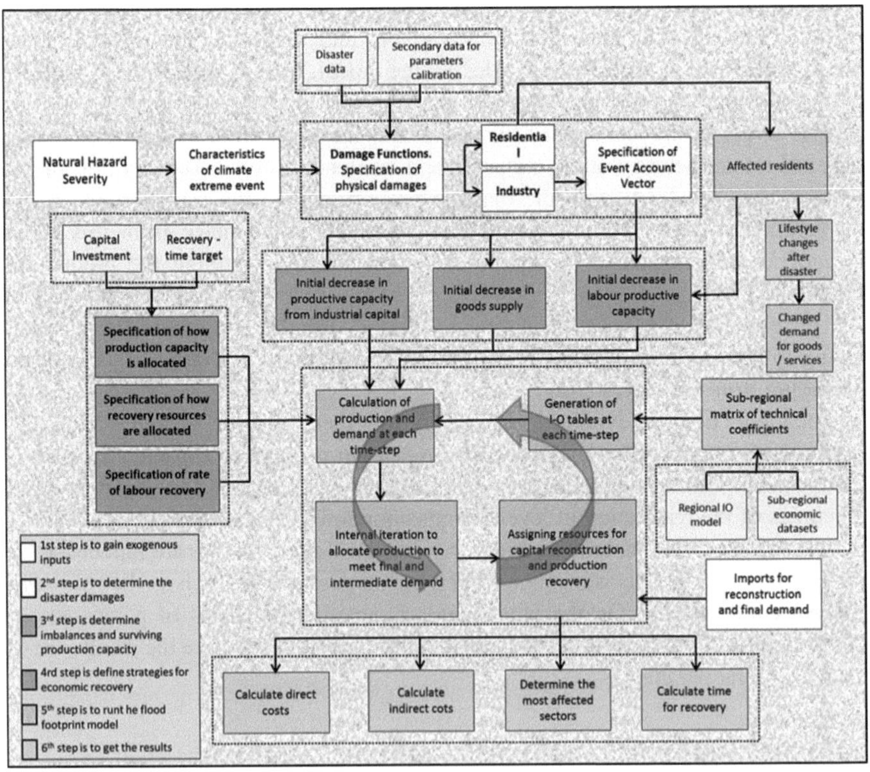

Fig. 3.1 Modelling process for flood footprint appraisal. (*Source*: Authors' own elaboration)

to pre-disaster levels. One can model the differences (e.g. costs and benefits) of economic costs *with* versus *without* any adaptation plans for future events in a city or country.

- Damage database and secondary information for parameters calibration (top white boxes) is the necessary information that constitutes the specification of the physical damages. When assessing past events, most of this information should be available from insurance or reinsurance companies. Other data sources for past events can be governmental reports and independent research reports (Penning-Rowsell et al. 2013). For future events, hydrological or flooding engineering models can be built into this damage database. For instance, flood inundation models would be able to predict duration and velocity of a flood event with inputs from predicted precipitation levels of climatic change models.
- The regional IO model (right-middle white box) provides annual input-output tables for the flood footprint model, and a subregional economic dataset allows us to construct the subregional IO tables. Most input-output tables are compiled and published at the national level. Some cities have city-level input-output tables. If there are no regional/city-specific input-output tables, statistical techniques, such as the location quotients method, can be applied to obtain such tables. In recent years, multiregional input-output (MRIO) models have been developed and extensively used. Utilisation of MRIO models in estimating economic costs in post-disaster situations has been limited and requires careful design and implementation in terms of estimating impacts to international/intraregional supply chains, which is the goal of this book.

Step 2 Determine the damages (in economic terms) caused by the destruction in residential and industrial capital (yellow boxes).

- After damage data is obtained from various sources, *damage functions* are constructed. Capital damage is categorised as industrial *capital* and *residential* capital. During recovery, both capitals will be repaired or replaced, but only industrial capital damage would affect economic productivity performance. In most cases, damage is reported in monetary terms. This needs to be converted to a proportion of damage in the industrial capital stock. This information is the input to construct the EAV.
- Damages to *residential capital* affect the economy in different ways (light orange boxes): from the production side, it affects the availability of the labour force. In addition, from the demand side, the consumption of the affected labour would change during a disaster aftermath.
- *Household consumption behaviour*: During a disaster and its recovery period, household demand for goods and services can change. For instance, households may keep the same consumption level for food and clothes (or basic needs) but may reduce the consumption of luxury goods and services. After the recovery, their consumption level for luxury goods and services could then return to pre-disaster levels. However, there is a lack of studies quantifying the relationship between consumption levels and disaster severity and recovery for different types

of disasters. Potential links with psychological studies could be an option here. Consumption behaviour in the aftermath of disasters might be exogenously modelled. Several assumptions regarding recovery paths have been tested to account for different situations. The analysis showed that the results are not very sensitive to changes in household consumption.

Step 3 Define the initial economic imbalances and the surviving production capacity after a disaster.

- *Labour constraint*: This can be obtained from the damage dataset, residential damage, and the number of affected households (or population). This information can be used to estimate the amount of labour which would be either unavailable or delayed when traveling to work, serving as a production constraint during the economic recovery period. However, there is a lack of studies related to determining the relationship between residential capital damage and labour delays, and some assumptions are tested in this book to model an exogenously labour recovery path. Data on labour constraints may be inferred from secondary data (such as from reports of governments or social organisations, or from the news). The information is cross-referenced with damages in some sectors that may affect labour productivity, such as residential damage and damages in the transport sectors.
- The remaining industrial capital and labour availability after the disaster will both affect the remaining production capacity. The minimum of the proportion of these two productive factors can be used to determine the remaining production capacity for economic recovery, as described in more detail in the IO model outline (see Eq. 3.11).

Step 4 Define the strategies for economic recovery during the disaster aftermath.

- Flood footprint modelling allows for carrying out some elements of recovery planning. In the flood footprint model, the recovery path for industrial capital accounts for the capital investment needed for each period to replace the value of the capital lost because of the disaster. In these cases, this model has shown that even when this capital is replaced, the economy may take longer to recover and some imbalances caused by the initial shock may remain longer.
- A rationing scheme is set up to determine priority levels for resource allocation, along with choosing specific recovery patterns for labour recovery, as well.
- An exogenous recovery path for labour based on the overall scale of the disaster is applied. We assume every labourer works for 8 × 22 h per month. If the number of extra hours for each labourer spent travelling per month t post-disaster replaces working hours, this is captured by o_i, and the percentage of labour affected is p_i, then the relative percentage of lost labour in the month is identified by: $p_i * o_i/(8 \times 22)$ (Li et al. 2013).

Step 5 Configure the flood footprint model and compute the recovery of the economy. The four boxes in the loop described in detail in the section above refers to the *recovery process*.

- After obtaining the regional technical coefficients matrix, the values for the regional input-output tables at each period are obtained directly. One can argue that such technical matrices can be changed after a disaster event due to new industrial relationships developed, but this information might not be available, in which case it could be assumed that both the production technology and the patterns throughout the recovery period remain constant. This assumption can only be reasonable if any disaster is not severe enough to allow immediate structural transformation of the production system, e.g., within a 1-year period.
- Production capacity and final demand recovery are calculated at each period.
- Calculated production capacity will be used as available resources to be allocated in the next period. The rationing scheme is applied to allocate the production capacity among intermediate-demand and all final-demand users.
- At every period, some damaged capital is recovered, and more production capacity is gained. The model will be looped until the pre-disaster production condition is met, both in level and equilibrium.
- In flood footprint modelling, it is assumed that imports contribute to some extent to the recovery process and to the supply of final consumption. The amount of imports may rely on the condition of the transportation sectors, as stated in the section on *Imports*. In modelling practice, we assume that the availability of required inputs from imports is as much as the pre-disaster level but constrained by the *transportation capacity*.

Step 6 Obtain the results from the flood footprint model. Four major results can be obtained, as shown in boxes at the bottom of Fig. 3.1.

- Direct economic costs (by industry and region) computed as the value added needed to replace the proportion of industrial capital that was destroyed by the disaster.
- Indirect economic costs (by industry and region) computed as the accumulation in each period of the difference between recovered production capacity, and the pre-disaster production level during the recovery time.
- The total economic costs, or flood footprint, is the sum of direct and indirect economic costs.
- The time taken to achieve full recovery.
- The results can be illustrated by industries and regions for the multiregional analysis.

3.1.4 Regionalisation of IO Technical Coefficients

As damages from disasters usually affect specific regions within a national context and given that most IO tables are available only at the national level, it has been the case that the regionalisation of the IO has been necessary within the FFA. This section describes the process followed to obtain the regional matrices for regional cases.

Several techniques have been developed within the IO analysis field to *regionalise* the technical coefficients, but statistical techniques are the most widely used.[5] Here, we use the Augmented Flegg Location Quotients (AFLQ) technique (Flegg and Webber 2000; Miller and Blair 2009; Romero et al. 2012) to obtain the regional IO coefficients matrix for our case studies. This technique seeks to correct the national technical coefficients to depict regional technology, given the regional economic structure.

For this purpose, economic data on the *local* economy is used to rescale the national coefficients, especially for employment, as this is one of the most reliable and available data sources at the subnational level. This process consists of adjusting the national coefficients to the regional scale by evaluating the relative size and technology of each industry in the regional economy in relation to national size. Some parameters are also adjusted to consider commercial traffic between the regional economy and other regions and the possible specialisation of an industry within the region.

Then, the regional technical coefficient, r_{ij}, is derived from the national technical coefficients, a_{ij}, when resized by a regional-economy parameter or *location quotient*, lq_{ij}, such as in Eq. 3.17:

$$r_{ij} = lq_{ij} * a_{ij} \tag{3.17}$$

where r_{ij} is the amount of input from industry i needed to produce one unit of output in industry j. Here, we apply one of the most widely used location quotients, lq_{ij}, the AFLQ. We depart from the simple location quotients (SLQ) to assess the relative importance of each regional industry i, as described in Eq. 3.18:

$$\mathrm{SLQ}_i = \frac{\mathrm{RE}_i/\mathrm{TRE}}{\mathrm{NE}_i/\mathrm{TNE}} \equiv \frac{\mathrm{RE}_i}{\mathrm{NE}_i} * \frac{\mathrm{TNE}}{\mathrm{TRE}} \tag{3.18}$$

where TRE is total employment in the region, TNE is total employment in the country, RE_i is employment of the supplying industry, and NE_i accounts for national employment in the same industry.

Then, the cross-industry LQ (CILQ) is derived from the SLQ to assess the relative importance of a supplier industry i regarding the purchasing industry j (see Eq. 3.19):

$$\mathrm{CILQ}_{ij} = \frac{\mathrm{RE}_i/\mathrm{NE}_i}{\mathrm{RE}_j/\mathrm{NE}_j} \equiv \frac{\mathrm{SLQ}_i}{\mathrm{SLQ}_j} * \frac{\mathrm{TNE}}{\mathrm{TRE}} \tag{3.19}$$

[5] It has been argued that survey-based techniques are more accurate, although the main difficulty of these types of analyses is that they are highly consuming of time and resources. On the other hand, statistical techniques offer a quick and cheap alternative without losing much accuracy (Romero et al. 2012).

Later, Flegg and Webber (2000) refined the regionalisation in the Flegg LQ (FLQ) to correct for the persistent underestimation of regional imports in the CILQ through the parameter $\lambda = [1 + \text{TRE/TNE}\ ]^{\delta}$ to obtain the FLQ. Finally, in the AFLQ (Eq. 3.20), one last parameter was added to cover the possibility of regional specialisation in some sectors, $\log_2(1 + \text{SLQ}_j)$:

$$\text{AFLQ}_{ij} \equiv \text{CILQ}_{ij} * \lambda * [\log_2(1 + \text{SLQ}_j)] \tag{3.20}$$

This generates a quotient for each of the elements in the national matrix of technical coefficients, A. Then, the regional matrix of technical quotients, A_{reg}, is:

$$A_{\text{reg}} = \text{AFLQ}. * A \tag{3.21}$$

3.2 Methodology for the Multiregional Flood Footprint Analysis (MFFA)

Up to this point, the rationale of modelling the total economic costs from disasters has been described. However, the analysis has been done considering the costs incurred within the national boundaries, i.e., within the boundaries of a national economy. However, the intricate linkages of national economies in a globalised world produce economic *resonances* in the entire world economic system from phenomena in whichever part of the world disasters might occur. Within this context, economic impact analysis must include effects on the global value chain, as well. To this end, a multiregional multinational model is developed which considers those rippled effects, as detailed below.

3.2.1 *The Model*

The multiregional version of the flood footprint model incorporates a multiregional IO (MRIO) table to account for the effects of changes in trade between an affected country and other countries because of production losses (see Sect. 2.4.2).

To incorporate the multiregional dimension to equations, let the superscript r refers to the region and goes before the superscript of time t. In case the origin and destiny region are needed, these will be indicated by either the superscript r or s (as in the expression $z^{rs,\,t}$) where the superscript to the left indicates the region of origin and the superscript to the right indicates the destiny region. In the case of final demand, the subscript k indicates the category in which the final demand is consumed, which may take the values: 1 (household demand), 2 (government consumption), 3 (capital investment), and 4 (exports). When considering this category, the

	Interregional interindustry consumption			Interregional final demand	Total output
	$\begin{bmatrix} z^{11}_{11} & z^{11}_{12} \\ z^{11}_{21} & z^{11}_{22} \end{bmatrix}$	$\begin{bmatrix} z^{12}_{11} & z^{12}_{12} \\ z^{12}_{21} & z^{12}_{22} \end{bmatrix}$	$\begin{bmatrix} z^{13}_{11} & z^{13}_{12} \\ z^{13}_{21} & z^{13}_{22} \end{bmatrix}$	$\begin{bmatrix} f^{11}_{1} & f^{12}_{1} & f^{13}_{1} \\ f^{11}_{2} & f^{12}_{2} & f^{13}_{2} \end{bmatrix}$	$\begin{bmatrix} x^{1}_{1} \\ x^{1}_{2} \end{bmatrix}$
	$\begin{bmatrix} z^{21}_{11} & z^{21}_{12} \\ z^{21}_{21} & z^{21}_{22} \end{bmatrix}$	$\begin{bmatrix} z^{22}_{11} & z^{22}_{12} \\ z^{22}_{21} & z^{22}_{22} \end{bmatrix}$	$\begin{bmatrix} z^{23}_{11} & z^{23}_{12} \\ z^{23}_{21} & z^{23}_{22} \end{bmatrix}$	$\begin{bmatrix} f^{21}_{1} & f^{22}_{1} & f^{23}_{1} \\ f^{21}_{2} & f^{22}_{2} & f^{23}_{2} \end{bmatrix}$	$\begin{bmatrix} x^{2}_{1} \\ x^{2}_{2} \end{bmatrix}$
	$\begin{bmatrix} z^{31}_{11} & z^{31}_{12} \\ z^{31}_{21} & z^{31}_{22} \end{bmatrix}$	$\begin{bmatrix} z^{32}_{11} & z^{32}_{12} \\ z^{32}_{21} & z^{32}_{22} \end{bmatrix}$	$\begin{bmatrix} z^{33}_{11} & z^{33}_{12} \\ z^{33}_{21} & z^{33}_{22} \end{bmatrix}$	$\begin{bmatrix} f^{31}_{1} & f^{32}_{1} & f^{33}_{1} \\ f^{31}_{2} & f^{32}_{2} & f^{33}_{2} \end{bmatrix}$	$\begin{bmatrix} x^{3}_{1} \\ x^{3}_{2} \end{bmatrix}$
Value added	$[va^1_1 \quad va^1_2]$	$[va^2_1 \quad va^2_2]$	$[va^3_1 \quad va^3_2]$		
Total inputs	$[x^1_1 \quad x^1_2]$	$[x^2_1 \quad x^2_2]$	$[x^3_1 \quad x^3_2]$		

Fig. 3.2 MRIO table for three regions with two sectors each. (*Source*: Based on Timmer et al. 2015)

subscript will be located to the right of the industry subscript (as in the expression $f_{i,\,k}$). Finally, the flooded region is distinguished by an asterisk next to the region superscript (as in the expression x^{r^*}).

The MRIO tables present the inter-industrial transactions within the regional economy, r, and the rest of the regions. Furthermore, the tables describe the flow of final products from region r to satisfy local and interregional final demand. Figure 3.2 presents an example of a MRIO table with three regions with the two same industries in each region.

Let us now reintroduce the mathematics of the MRIO, following the related description stated before. The general structure that describes the MRIO model, as in Eq. 3.22 (reproduced here), is:

$$x = CAx + Cf. \tag{3.22}$$

Note that the elements in Eq. 3.22 contains the information for all regions. To avoid confusion, we redefine the terms so that $CA = A^R$, $Cf = \tilde{f}i = f^R$, where i is a *summation* vector (a vector of ones) with same number of elements as columns in matrix $\tilde{f}$. Likewise, x^R is the production (transposed) vector for all regions, i.e., $x^R = [x^1, x^2, \ldots, x^r, \ldots, x^q]$ where q is the number of regions, and the superscript R indicates an element that encloses the information for all regions. Note that all the elements contain the information of all sectors of the correspondent region.

The model now looks similar to the original single-region IO:

$$x^R = A^R x^R + f^R. \tag{3.23}$$

Hereafter, for simplicity, let us assume all regions have the same number of sectors (which is the case with the data used here). Therefore, vector x^R and vector f^R have dimensions of $(n * q) \times 1$, and the matrix A^R has a dimension $(n * q) \times (n * q)$, so the resulting vector $A^R x^R$ has a dimension $(n * q) \times 1$. Here, n is the total number of industries in each region, and q is the total number of regions.

When expanded, this can be written as:

$$\begin{bmatrix} x^1 \\ \vdots \\ x^r \\ \vdots \\ x^R \end{bmatrix} = \begin{bmatrix} A^{11} & \dots & A^{1R} \\ \vdots & A^{rs} & \vdots \\ A^{r1} & A^{rr} & A^{rR} \\ \vdots & \ddots & \vdots \\ A^{R1} & \dots & A^{RR} \end{bmatrix} \begin{bmatrix} x^1 \\ \vdots \\ x^r \\ \vdots \\ x^R \end{bmatrix} + \begin{bmatrix} f^{11} & \dots & f^{1R} \\ \vdots & f^{rs} & \vdots \\ f^{r1} & f^{rr} & f^{rR} \\ \vdots & \ddots & \vdots \\ f^{R1} & \dots & f^{RR} \end{bmatrix} \begin{bmatrix} I \\ \vdots \\ I \\ \vdots \\ I \end{bmatrix} \tag{3.24}$$

where x^r is the vector of production in region r (with dimension $n \times 1$). A^{rs} is the matrix $\widehat{c}^{rs} A^r$ in Eq. (2.18) that indicates the technical proportion of goods produced in region s needed for production in region r when $s \neq r$, and the regional technical coefficients matrix A^{rr} when $s = r$ (with dimension $n \times n$). On the other hand, f^{rs} is the vector of total final demand in region s for products from region r when $s \neq r$ (or final products exports from region r to region s), and the local final demand, f^{rr}, when $r = s$ (of dimension $n \times 1$). Therefore, the production of region r is:

$$x^r = \sum_s A^{rs} x^s + \sum_s f^{rs}. \tag{3.25}$$

Equation 3.25 expresses the product required by region r from all other regions, including both intermediate and final demand. Note that the summation operators run over regions, which indicates the summation of vectors.

On the other hand, the (transposed) vector of technical coefficients of labour in the multiregional version of the *basic equation* (Eq. 3.26) contains the labour data for all industries and all regions:

$$l^{R\prime} = \begin{bmatrix} \left(\frac{l_1^1}{x_1^1}, \frac{l_2^1}{x_2^1}, \dots, \frac{l_i^1}{x_i^1}, \dots, \frac{l_n^1}{x_n^1}\right), \dots, \left(\frac{l_1^r}{x_1^r}, \frac{l_2^r}{x_2^r}, \dots, \frac{l_i^r}{x_i^r}, \dots, \frac{l_n^r}{x_n^r}\right), \dots, \\ \left(\frac{l_1^q}{x_1^q}, \frac{l_2^q}{x_2^q}, \dots, \frac{l_i^q}{x_i^q}, \dots, \frac{l_n^q}{x_n^q}\right) \end{bmatrix} \tag{3.26}$$

where the element $\left[\frac{l_i^r}{x_i^r}\right]$ indicates the technical proportion of labour required in region r in industry i to produce one unit of product in the same region and industry.

From this point, the model proceeds in an analogous way to the flood footprint single-regional model described in Sect. 3.1.

3.2.2 *Main Constraints*

3.2.2.1 Production Constraints

The development of the multiregional version of the model allows for the assessment of different disasters happening at the same time in different regions, or the same disaster affecting several regions. This is possible thanks to the multiregional EAV ($\gamma_{\text{cap}}^{R,t}$) and the analogous element to consider constraints in labour productive capacity ($\gamma_1^{R,t}$). For simplicity, this case examines a single extreme climate event in one region (r^*).

3.2.2.2 Labour Productivity Constraints

Like the standard IO model, the productive capacity given the labour constraints at each period is:

$$x_l^{R,t} = \left[\left(i - \gamma_l^{R,t}\right)\right] .* x^{R,0} \tag{3.27}$$

where the term $\gamma_l^{R,t}$ is a vector of dimension $(n * r) \times 1$ and contains the proportion of affected productive capacity owing to labour constraints in industry i in region r for each period of the recovery. The element i is a vector of ones the same size as vector γ_l^t. The term $x^{R,\,0}$ is the vector of production in all sectors in all regions prior to the disaster:

$$\gamma_l^{\prime R,t} = \begin{array}{l}\left[\left(0_{l,1}, \ldots, 0_{l,i}, .., 0_{l,i}\right)^1, \ldots, \left(\gamma_{l,1}, \ldots, \gamma_{l,i}, \ldots, \gamma_{l,n}\right)^{r^*}, \ldots,\right. \\ \left.\left(0_{l,1}, \ldots, 0_{l,i}, \ldots, 0_{l,n}\right)^q\right]^t.\end{array} \tag{3.28}$$

The vectors in parenthesis indicate the damage by sector in each region, so that for non-flooded regions, the damage from labour constraints is zero.

3.2.3 Production Constraints by Capital

Like labour constraints, the multiregional EAV ($\gamma_{\text{cap}}^{R,t}$) is a vector of dimension $(n * r) \times 1$ that contains the proportions of affected industrial capital in each sector in each affected region, at the period t. Assuming just region r has been affected by a disaster, the multiregional EAV will account for the reduced production capacity due to damage of industrial capital in region r^* and will contain zeros in the rest of the elements, as in Eq. 3.29 (note the presentation is in row form):

$$\gamma_{\text{cap}}^{R,t} = \begin{bmatrix} \left(0_{\text{cap},1}, \ldots, 0_{\text{cap},i}, .., 0_{\text{cap},n}\right)^1, \ldots, \\ \left(\gamma_{\text{cap},1}, \ldots, \gamma_{\text{cap},i}, \ldots, \gamma_{\text{cap},n}\right)^{r^*}, \ldots, \left(0_{\text{cap},1}, \ldots, 0_{\text{cap},i}, \ldots, 0_{\text{cap},n}\right)^q \end{bmatrix}^t \tag{3.29}$$

As in the case of labour constraints, the vector of available production capacity of industrial capital in time t for all industries and all regions is given in a transposed way by Eq. 3.30. This is a (transposed) vector of dimension $(n * q) \times 1$ and indicates the constraints in the affected region(s) wherein the elements have a positive value ($\gamma_i^{r,t} > 0$):

$$\begin{aligned} x_{\text{cap}}^{R,t} &= \left(i - \gamma_{\text{cap}}^{R}\right). * x^{R,0} \\ &= \left[(x_1, \ldots, x_n)^1, \ldots, ((1-\gamma_1)x_1, \ldots, (1-\gamma_n)x_n)^{r^*}, \ldots (x_1, \ldots, x_n)^q\right]^t \end{aligned} \tag{3.30}$$

3.2.4 Changes in Final Demand

The changes in final demand for the affected region are modelled as in the single-regional model, while the rest of the regions remain unchanged. The final demand in the affected region changes by two factors that act in opposite directions. First, behavioural changes in household consumption reduce the local demand for those non-basic products/industries, but local demand remains the same for the industries providing basic goods.[6] Secondly, the final demand increases in those industries locally involved in the reconstruction process.

[6]Note that here it is assumed that just the local demand is reduced, while imports for non-basic products remain available at the same rate. This assumption is applied following (Li et al. 2013).

3.2.5 Post-disaster Recovery Process

The process to determine the production capacity in the aftermath of a disaster works in the same way as in the single-region model for the affected region. Then, the productive capacity of industrial capital is compared to the productive capacity of labour to determine the economy's capacity, as in Eq. 3.31.

Then, the *rationing scheme* is conducted in the same way as in the single-regional model to determine any possible bottleneck in the supply chain. After this, the total production capacity of the affected region is determined, and together with the adapted final demand, the level of total demand is determined for the affected region each period t:

$$x_{td}^{r^*,t} = \sum_s A^{rs^*} x_{tp}^{r^*,t} + \sum_s f^{r^*s,t} \tag{3.31}$$

where the first summation ($\sum_s A^{rs^*} x_{tp}^{r^*,t}$) is the sum of vectors of dimension $n \times 1$, each of them representing the intermediate inputs from each region s needed to produce in region r^*. The second summation ($\sum_s f^{r^*s,t}$) is the sum of vectors of dimension $n \times 1$, each of them representing the total final demand that each region s demands for products from region r^*. Note that the intermediate demand in the MRIO table, $A^{r^*s} x^{r^*,t}$, accounts for the intermediate inputs from region r^* that are needed for production in each another region s when $r^* \neq s$ (or exports for intermediate demand products), and it represents the local intermediate demand when $s = r^*$. Likewise, final demand, $f^{r^*s,}$, considers the local final demand when $s = r^*$, and the demand of other regions for products of region r^* when $s \neq r^*$.

For each point in time, the vector of total demand for all regions includes this *new* final demand (household-adapted demand and recovery demand) for the affected region ($x_{td}^{r^*,t}$). The vector of total demand for all industries and all regions has the dimension $(n * q) \times 1$:

$$x_{td}^{t} = \begin{bmatrix} x_{td}^{1,t} \\ x_{td}^{2,t} \\ \vdots \\ x_{td}^{r^*,t} \\ \vdots \\ x_{td}^{q,t} \end{bmatrix} \tag{3.32}$$

where each element $x_{td}^{r,t}$ is a vector of dimension $n \times 1$ that accounts for the final demand of region r. In the MFFA model, it is precisely the vector of total demand for all regions that is the source of changes in production in the other regions different from r^*. It accounts for changes in total demand in the affected region ($x^{r^*,t}$) and, in consequence, the changes in intermediate production of all suppliers of region r^*, local and external. The new vector of production for all regions is:

$$x^t = Ax^t_{td} + \sum_s f^{s,t} \tag{3.33}$$

where each vector f^s of dimension $(n * q) \times 1$ accounts for the total final demand in region s of products from all other regions, including the local final demand in s:

$$f^{s,t} = \begin{bmatrix} f^{1s} \\ \vdots \\ f^{ss} \\ \vdots \\ f^{r^*s} \\ \vdots \\ f^{qs} \end{bmatrix}^{t.} \tag{3.34}$$

Note that the vector of final demand influences the total demand only in the affected region r^*, although this is an assumption that can be modified in the model. Nevertheless, determining the distribution of the reduction in external consumption would imply more assumptions.

The total production of each region r at each period during the recovery is, then:

$$\begin{aligned} x^{r,t} &= \sum_s A^{rs,t} x^{s,t}_{td} + \sum_s f^{rs,t} \\ &= \left[A^{r1} x^1_{td} + \ldots + A^{rs} x^s_{td} + \ldots + A^{rs^*} x^{s^*}_{td} + \ldots + A^{sq} x^q_{td}\right]^t \\ &\quad + \left[f^{r1} + \ldots + f^{rs} + \ldots + f^{rq}\right]^t \end{aligned} \tag{3.35}$$

where each element of the summation ($A^{rs}x^s_{td}$) is the $n \times 1$ vector of intermediate inputs that each region s needs from region r.

The indirect costs in each non-flooded region, s, in each period are determined by the difference in the production level accounting for the effects in decreasing intermediate demand from the affected region and the pre-disaster level:

$$va^{s,t}_{\text{ind}} = x^{s,0} - x^{s,t} = A^{sr^*} x^{r^*,0}_{td} - A^{sr^*} x^{r^*,t}_{td}. \tag{3.36}$$

Finally, the total flood footprint (ff) for all regions considers the direct costs in the affected region ($va^{r^*}_{\text{dir}}$), the indirect costs in the affected region ($va^{r^*}_{\text{ind}}$), and the indirect costs to the rest of the regions ($\sum_{s \neq r^*} va^s_{\text{ind}}$):

$$ff_{mr} = va_{\text{dir}}^{r^*} + va_{\text{ind}}^{r^*} + \sum_{s \neq r^*} va_{\text{ind}}^{s}$$

$$= f_{\text{rec}}^{r^*,0} + \left(T^{r^*}\left(x^{r^*,0}\right) - \sum\nolimits_t x_{tp}^{r^*,t}\right) + \sum_{s \neq r^*}\left(T^{s}\left(x^{s,0}\right) - \sum\nolimits_t x_{tp}^{s,t}\right). \tag{3.37}$$

3.3 Final Remarks

This chapter provides the entire modelling of the MFFA, following the modelling rationale for single-region analysis, to arrive at the final multiregional version of the model. MFFA can be useful for the investigation of the spatial and industrial distribution of the indirect economic impacts of disasters.

The MFFA models three types of changes: (a) changes in production caused by destruction in industrial, residential, and infrastructure capital, (b) disruptions in production capacity due to constraints in labour availability, and (c) behavioural changes in final consumption. Furthermore, it provides a roadmap for recovery dynamics through time. Since it is based on IO analysis, the appraisal is performed at the industrial level and with a multiregional dimension. The model is compatible with other integration techniques, such as flood modelling and geographical information systems (GIS) analysis. The possibilities presented by the use of the MFFA might bring greater precision, prompter results, and scenario analysis.

A multiregional model in disaster analysis is very necessary given the populations and industries at risk in different locations around the world which would propagate the economic impacts caused by a regional disruption. The following chapter presents results of the MFFA applied to several disaster cases.

Chapter 4
Case Applications

The objective of this chapter is to apply the FFA to four cases. The first is the single-region version of the model applied to a real past event: the 2007 floods in Yorkshire and the Humber, UK. The second case is an application of the same model to an event that affected several regions within Europe. The third constitutes an application to quantify potential benefits of risk management strategies, considered as avoided costs due to the implementation of blue-green infrastructure in the City of Newcastle, UK. The fourth and last case study is the application of the multiregional model to a projected scenario of development and climate change for the city of Rotterdam, the Netherlands. This last case represents the main model application of the book.

4.1 Single-Region FFA: The Case of the 2007 Floods in Yorkshire and the Humber, UK[1]

This section shows the model's outcomes for an empirical case and points out lessons for modelling improvements in following stages. In this case, the analysis covers a single region, which commonly corresponds to political or economic demarcations within a country, as data availability was collected in these terms.

[1]For a fuller description of the model's application to this case study, please refer to Mendoza-Tinoco et al. (2017).

© The Author(s), under exclusive license to Springer Nature Switzerland AG 2023

D. Mendoza-Tinoco et al., *Multiregional Flood Footprint Analysis*, SpringerBriefs in Economics, https://doi.org/10.1007/978-3-031-29728-1_4

4.1.1 The Floods

The 2007 summer floods in the UK were selected as a case study for demonstration purposes to show the primary modelling stages of the MFFA. They were chosen based on their relevance as some of the major flooding events in the century, causing a major civil emergency nationwide in the UK. Unfortunately, there were 13 deaths and approximately 7000 people had to be rescued from the flooded areas. Over 55,000 properties were flooded and over half a million people experienced shortages of water and electricity in the country (Pitt 2008). We selected Yorkshire and the Humber (Y&H) as the analysis region (see Fig. 4.1), as it was the most affected region during the event. The damages in the region accounted for 65.5% of the direct damage nationally, where several businesses, schools, and public buildings were flooded and infrastructure services such as roads and electricity substations suffered significant disruptions.

4.1.1.1 Data Gathering and Codification

This section describes the data collecting process for the analysis. All the data was collected or regionalised when needed for the Y&H region, coded under the NUT2[2] classification. All values are for 2007, and when monetary, they are in millions of British pounds (£million) in 2009 prices. A monthly time scale was used for the temporal analysis, and the sectoral disaggregation used 46 economic sectors (see Table 4.1).

The flood footprint model requires two sets of data: economic data about the affected region and information about the disaster.

4.1.1.2 Economic Data

The economic data includes information on employment, capital stock, and the IO tables. The economic information for employment, final consumption, and output comes from the UK Multisectoral Dynamic Model (MDM) by Cambridge Econometrics Ltd.,[3] a macro-econometric model used to analyse and forecast environmental, energy, and economic data for the 12 NUTS2 regions in the UK.

The regional matrix of technical coefficients, **A**, was obtained from the UK matrix using the technique of location quotients described in the methodology section.

[2] According to the Eurostat organisation, "The NUTS classification (nomenclature of territorial units for statistics) is a hierarchical system for dividing up the economic territory of the EU for the purpose of: The collection, development and harmonisation of European regional statistics, socio-economic analyses of the regions, and framing of EU regional policies" (http://ec.europa.eu/eurostat/web/nuts/overview).

[3] http://www.camecon.com/how/mdm-e3-model/

Fig. 4.1 Yorkshire and the Humber region within the UK. (*Source*: Transport Planning Society, https://tps.org.uk/regions-nations/yorkshire-humber)

4.1.1.3 Disaster Data

Ideally, the disaster data for the flood footprint model should comprise information of damages to capital (industrial, residential, and infrastructure), reductions in labour capacity, and changes in final demand. The information on damages to capital would conform to the event account vector (EAV). For labour effects, some assumptions are considered for an exogenous modelling of labour damage and recovery. The

Table 4.1 EAV for the 2007 floods in Y&H

Industrial sector	£Million	% Direct damage to capital stock	Industrial sector	£Million	% Direct damage to capital stock
Agriculture, etc.	1.0	0.001%	Land transport	71.4	0.019%
Mining and quarrying	1.0	0.001%	Water transport	13.4	0.047%
Food, drink, and tobacco	15.3	0.009%	Air transport	13.4	0.025%
Textiles, etc.	14.6	0.026%	Warehousing and postal	7.3	0.001%
Wood and paper	15.0	0.089%	Accommodation	7.2	0.135%
Printing and recording	15.5	0.009%	Food and beverage services	7.3	0.014%
Coke and petroleum	15.2	0.031%	Media	7.5	0.007%
Chemicals, etc.	15.5	0.011%	IT services	94.4	0.231%
Pharmaceuticals	15.4	0.041%	Financial and insurance	24.1	0.012%
Non-metals	14.6	0.009%	Real estate	24.4	0.031%
Metals	15.3	0.007%	Legal and accounting	0.5	0.033%
Computers, etc.	15.4	0.019%	Head offices and manage. co.	0.1	0.038%
Electrical equipment	14.7	0.022%	Architectural and related sectors	0.6	0.035%
Machinery, etc.	14.9	0.022%	Other professional services	2.7	0.032%
Motor vehicles, etc.	15.5	0.029%	Business support services	23.9	0.014%
Other transport. equipment	15.0	0.054%	PAD	41.4	0.009%
Other manuf. and repair	15.3	0.089%	Education	16.4	0.009%
Electricity and gas	91.4	0.014%	Health	39.4	0.064%
Water, sewerage, and waste	101.4	0.109%	Residential and social	1.0	0.011%
Construction	7.0	0.014%	Arts	1.0	0.047%
Motor vehicle trade	7.6	0.012%	Recreational services	1.0	0.004%
Wholesale trade	7.3	0.182%	Other services	1.0	0.004%
Retail trade	6.9	0.095%	Unallocated	0.0	0.000%

main data source for this case study is provided by the UK Environmental Agency in the report, 'Economic Impacts of Flood Risk on Yorkshire and Humber. Cost of 2007 Floods'.

For damages occurring to industrial capital, the report states that the total cost was £380 million for business premises, stock, equipment, etc. Additionally, £470 million in damages were sustained by *infrastructure* sectors, namely, transport, IT services, electricity and gas, water, sewerage and waste, PAD, education, and health sectors. As the sectoral disaggregation in the report is for 15 categories, an allocation of damage to each sector was made through a weighted distribution based on the relative weight of the sector in the regional economy. This data was compared to the stocks of industrial capital to determine the proportion of affected productive capacity, i.e. the value of the EAV as presented in Appendix A.

Regarding residential damage, 10,759 houses were reported to be flooded, which represents 0.6% of the total housing in the region. Total household damages were estimated as £340 million by the UK Environmental Agency.

Information on labour constraints is very scarce for this case, and the damaged labour was derived from the number of flooded houses multiplied by the average number of working people per household. Additionally, commuting delays were proportionally related to damage in the transport sectors. This resulted in a delay of 1 h in commuting for 1.5% of the working population.

Finally, as information on changes in final demand is very scarce, we followed a sensitivity analysis about different levels of reduction in non-basic products and about the diverse shapes of the recovery curves. The values for the analysis show a decrease of 0.25% in household demand for non-basic industries and a recovery time of 6 months with positive and marginally decreasing growth, i.e. a higher recovery rate for the first periods, which slowed down at the end of the recovery.

4.1.2 Model Results

4.1.2.1 Total Economic Losses for Yorkshire and the Humber Region

According to the flood footprint analysis, it should have taken at least 14 months for the regional economy to return to the pre-disaster situation after the extreme event (Fig. 4.2). This recovery entails both achieving economic equilibrium and returning to pre-disaster production levels. The total economic loss was calculated in £2.7 billion, which is equivalent to 3.9% of the annual gross value added of the region (GVA).

Figure 4.2 compares the shares of each category. The direct economic loss (industrial, residential, and infrastructure) accounts for 1.7% of the yearly GVA (nearly £1.2 billion), of which the majority corresponds to industrial and infrastructural damages (71%). The indirect economic costs (the non-realised production) account for an additional 2.2% of the regional GVA, at around £1.5 billion. This represents 56% of the total flood footprint.

Fig. 4.2 Flood footprint. Damage composition (£ million). (*Source*: Authors' own elaboration)

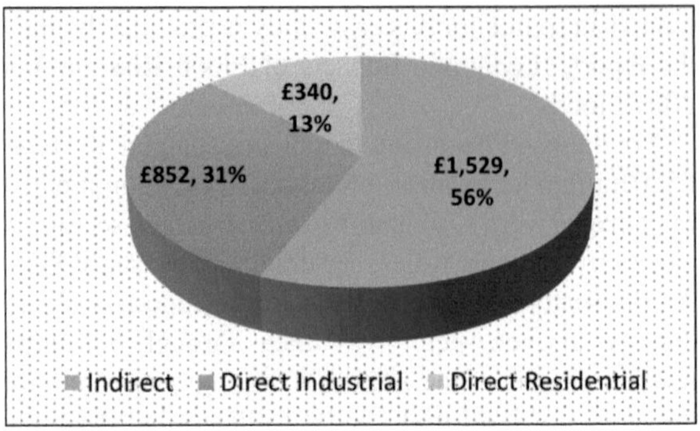

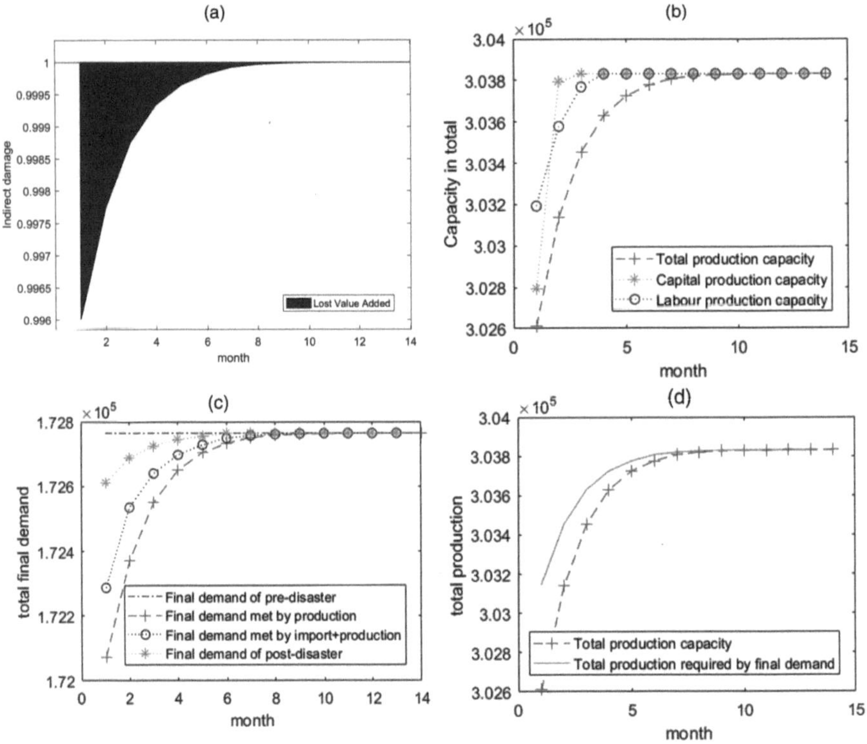

Fig. 4.3 Recovery process. (*Source*: Authors' own elaboration)

In the following, we present the progress of the economic variables involved in the recovery process.

Figure 4.3a depicts the cumulative damage in the recovery process. The area in purple, which indicates the distance between the final demand met by the available production at each time and the pre-disaster level, represents the total indirect damage over the course of the recovery process. The initial shock represents a decrease of 0.4% in total productive capacity. The shape of the curve shows a fast recovery in the beginning, especially in the first 4–5 months. It must be noted, however, that the recovery-curve shape is influenced by the rationing scheme chosen for the modelling, where the inter-industrial and recovery demand is prioritised over other final demands.

Figure 4.3b displays the recovery process of productive capacity, including both labour and industrial capital capacities. This figure indicates that industrial capital constraints constitute the main source of production disruptions in the first period after the disaster.

Figure 4.3c depicts the dynamics of the final demand in the recovery. The green line indicates the adaptation and recovery process of the final demand. This variable includes the adapted behaviour of final consumers and reconstruction demand. On the other hand, the red line shows how much of that adapted demand can be supplied by the actual constrained capacity of production. Part of the demand that cannot be satisfied by internal production is supplied through imports, as the black line illustrates.

Finally, Fig. 4.3d indicates the inequalities that remain between the level of production required by the final demand during the recovery process and the product supply from the surviving production capacity during the disaster's aftermath.

4.1.3 Sectoral Analysis

Because it is based on the IO model, one of the strengths of the flood footprint framework is the capacity to provide sectoral analysis. This is especially useful for disentangling the distribution of the knock-on effects as they propagate through the impacted economy and through other economic systems. Additionally, this capacity of the flood footprint framework becomes very convenient when planning for flood risk management and adaptation strategies.

Figure 4.4 shows the distribution of the flood footprint for both direct and indirect damage among ten industrial groups. The proportions of direct and indirect costs present high heterogeneity among the sector groups. For instance, manufacturing was shown to be the most affected sector, with a share of indirect costs that was 60% higher than direct costs, with the total damages in this group accounting for 23% of the total flood footprint. The utilities sector suffered major direct damages (£190 million), as infrastructure damages are allocated among this sector. The financial and professional sector was the most indirectly affected, with 21% of total indirect damages, while just 9% of total direct damages were concentrated in this group.

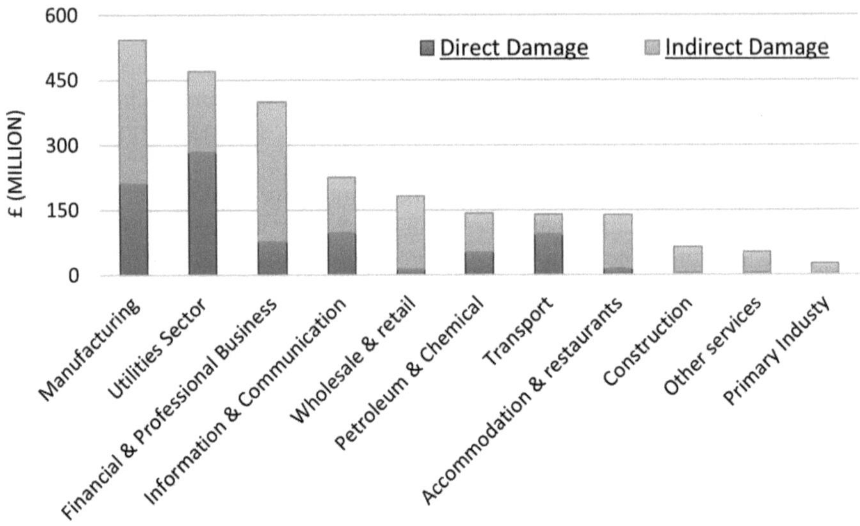

Fig. 4.4 Sectoral distribution of damage. (*Source*: Authors' own elaboration)

4.1.4 Case Summary

The flood footprint model was successfully applied to assess the total economic cost resulting from a real past event: the 2007 summer floods in the Yorkshire and the Humber region of the UK.

This constituted the first application of the flood footprint framework. The analysis supports the important lesson that losses from a disaster are exacerbated by economic mechanisms, that knock-on effects (or indirect damage) constitute a substantial proportion of total costs, and that some of the most affected sectors can be those that are not directly damaged. For this case study, the proportion of indirect damages accounts for over half of the total flood footprint. Neglecting the impact of indirect damages would hide the real social costs, especially in those sectors where direct damage is not very high.

There are, however, some caveats that must be noted. An impact assessment analysis is always subject to some degree of uncertainty. In this case, data scarcity is the main source of uncertainty, making the use of strong assumptions unavoidable in certain parameters.

For the disaster data, the following case studies incorporate the use of damage functions[4] and take advantage of the engineering flood modelling and GIS techniques that have recently evolved, providing more accurate sources of information.

[4] "Damage functions show the susceptibility of assets at risk to certain inundation characteristics, currently mostly against inundation depth" (Messner et al. 2007). This concept will be addressed in the next chapter.

Finally, although the model effectively accounts for knock-on effects in the affected regional economy, global economic interconnectedness requires moving the analysis to a multiregional approach if we are to make an exhaustive impact assessment.

4.2 Single-Region FFA for Multiple Regions: The Case of the 2010 Windstorm Xynthia in Europe

4.2.1 The Windstorm

In late February 2010, the powerful storm Xynthia from the Atlantic Ocean crossed Southern and Western Europe with strong winds up to 175 kmph, causing a rise in sea levels and heavy rainfall. It was the costliest disaster of 2010, which together with Windstorm Klaus (in the same year) resulted in 65 casualties and £4 billion in material damages (Triple E Consulting 2014). Figure 4.5 shows the area affected by the storm, as well as the direction and intensity of the winds in the different regions of Western and Southern Europe. The left side of the map shows the 82 NUTS2 regions considered for the analysis of this case study.

France was the country worst affected, with Belgium, Germany, Italy, Luxemburg, Spain, the Netherlands, and the UK also reporting casualties and material damages. The transport sectors were severely affected across the countries, including

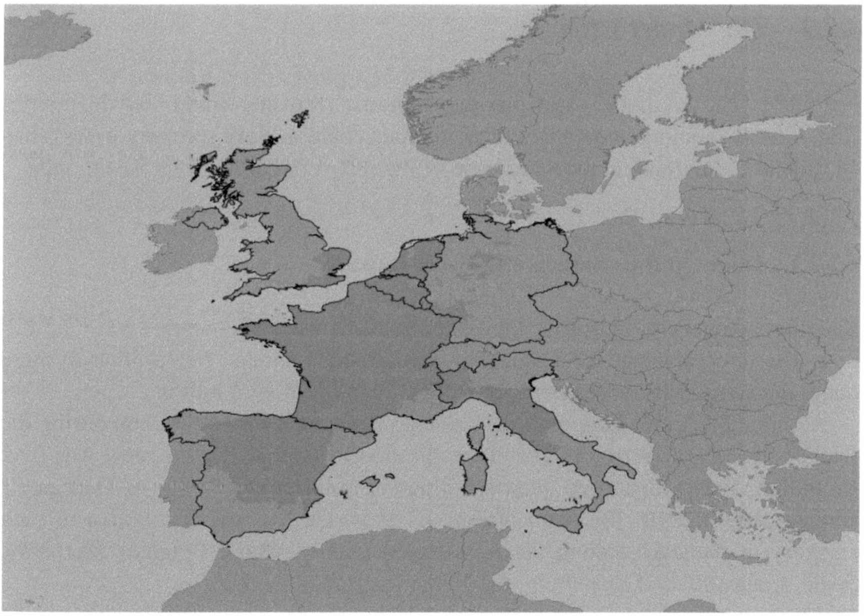

Fig. 4.5 Regions under the influence of the 2010 Xynthia windstorm. (*Source*: Authors' own elaboration with information from the GADM database (www.gadm.org))

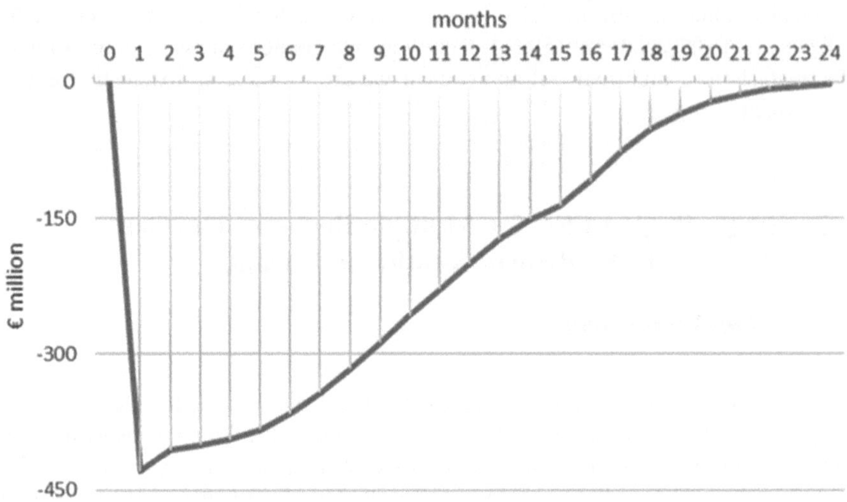

Fig. 4.6 Economic recovery path for the 2010 Xynthia windstorm. (*Source*: Authors' own elaboration)

roads, railways, and flights. Power stations and electric networks were badly damaged, leaving up to one million households without electricity for up to 3 days across the impacted regions, but especially in France.

4.2.2 *The Model's Results*

For this event, the model estimated the economy recovery would take 24 months (Fig. 4.6). It should be noted that some regions could achieve recovery in less than 24 months, explaining in part the shape of the recovery curve for the last months.

4.2.2.1 Direct and Cumulative Indirect Impacts

The direct damage to industrial capital in the eight affected countries was €2.5 billion. The direct damages to residential capital added another €1.7 billion to these direct damages. This represents a total direct damage of €4.2 billion.

Additionally, cumulative indirect damages accounted for €4.8 billion during the first 24 months of recovery. Therefore, the flood footprint for the event was over €9 billion. For comparative purposes, this is equivalent to 0.35% of Germany's annual GDP in 2010. The maps in Fig. 4.7 show the regional distribution of each category of damages among the 82 affected regions within Belgium, Germany, Spain, France, Italy, Luxemburg, the Netherlands, and the UK.

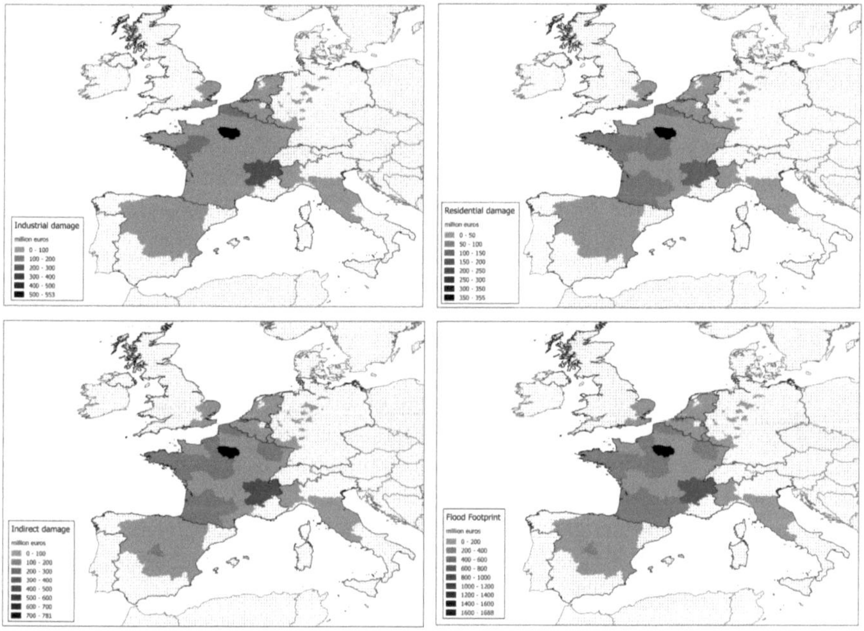

Fig. 4.7 Regional distribution of damages caused by the 2010 Xynthia windstorm. (*Source*: Authors' own elaboration)

4.2.2.2 Industrial Direct Damages

The upper-left map in Fig. 4.7a depicts the regional distribution of direct damages to industrial capital. France was the country worst affected, with 75% of the industrial direct damages (ca. €1.9 billion). The distribution of damages to industrial capital among other countries was as follows: Germany (16%), Spain (6%), and Belgium (3%). The remaining 1.3% was distributed among Italy, Luxembourg, the Netherlands, and the UK.

The worst affected region was Île-de-France, accounting for 29% of the industrial damages in France.

4.2.2.3 Residential Direct Damages

The upper-right Fig. 4.7 map (b) shows the direct damages to residential capital. Again, France was the most affected country, with 70% of the total damage in this category (ca. €1.2 billion). The three most affected regions were located within France: Île-de-France with 29%, Rhône-Alpes with 11%, and Nord-Pas-de-Calais with 6% of the French residential damage.

4.2.2.4 Indirect Damages

The regional distribution of the indirect damages is presented in the lower-left corner of Fig. 4.7c. The most affected country was France, accounting for 62% of total indirect damages (€3 billion), with Île-de-France being the most affected region, accounting for 26% of the indirect national damage (€780 million). The most affected regions outside France were Düsseldorf (€124 million), Germany, and Comunidad de Madrid (€120 million) in Spain.

4.2.2.5 Windstorm Footprint

The regional distribution of the flood footprint of this event is presented in the lower-right map in Fig. 4.7d. France concentrates the largest proportion of damages, with over two-thirds of the total flood footprint (€6 billion). Germany accounts for 18% (€1.7 billion), Spain, 7% (€610 million), Belgium, 3% (€307 million), Italy, 2% (€180 million), the Netherlands, 1.7% (€154 million), the UK, 0.7% (€61 million), and Luxemburg, 0.5% (€41 million). On average, the damages accounted for nearly 0.84% of each national GDP.

4.2.2.6 Sectoral Distribution

Figure 4.8 depicts direct and indirect damage organised by industrial sector for all affected regions. The most affected sectors by direct damage were utilities, business services, and general manufacturing sectors. These three sectors concentrate 46% of the total direct damages (€1.1 billion). Regarding indirect damages, the business services sector was the worst affected, accounting for 30% of the total indirect damages (€1.5 billion).

4.2.2.7 National Distribution of Damages by Industrial Sector

Figure 4.9 shows the national distribution by economic sector of direct and indirect damages. In all countries, the sector most affected by direct damages was the utilities. In the case of indirect damages, the three most affected sectors were business services, construction, and general manufacturing.

In France, direct damages to industrial capital accounted for €1.9 billion, while indirect damages accounted for €3 billion. Around 43% of direct damages were accounted for by utilities (€353 million), business services (€282 million), and the general manufacturing (€216 million) sectors. On the other hand, 71% of indirect damages were concentrated in business services (€931 million), construction (€613 million), and the general manufacturing (€559 million) sectors.

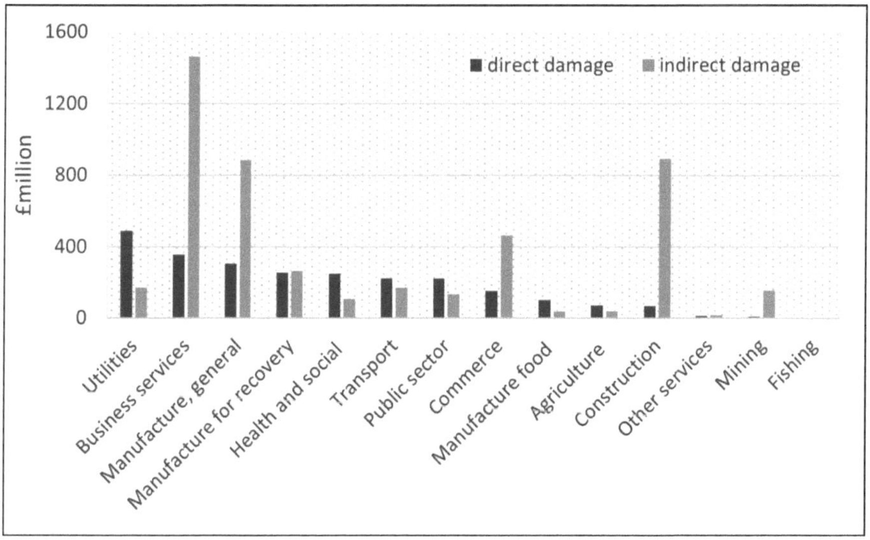

Fig. 4.8 Distribution of direct and indirect damage by economic sector. (*Source*: Authors' own elaboration)

In Germany, direct damages to industrial capital added €400 million and indirect damages accounted for €914 million. Three sectors, utilities (€85 million), manufacturing for recovery (€66 million), and general manufacturing (€55 million) concentrated 52% of the direct damages. Two-thirds of indirect damages were concentrated in business services (€267 million), general manufacturing (€186 million), and the construction (€152 million) sectors.

Direct damages in Spain accounted for €151 million, while indirect damages accounted for €360 million. Direct damages in utilities (€32.6 million) and general manufacturing (€20.5 million) represented 35% of the total. In comparison, business services, construction, and general manufacturing concentrated around two-thirds of the indirect damages (€226 million).

Belgium, Italy, Luxemburg, the Netherlands, and the UK, together, accounted for 4% of the direct damages (€100 million) and 12% of the indirect damages (€570 million).

4.2.3 Summary

The results for this case study show the regional distribution of the direct and indirect damages for a past extreme climate event. The single-regional footprint model, applied to multiple regions, allows consideration of the total economic impact of the disaster and the comparison of the differences in economic structures among regions. This analysis becomes especially useful in a context such as that of the

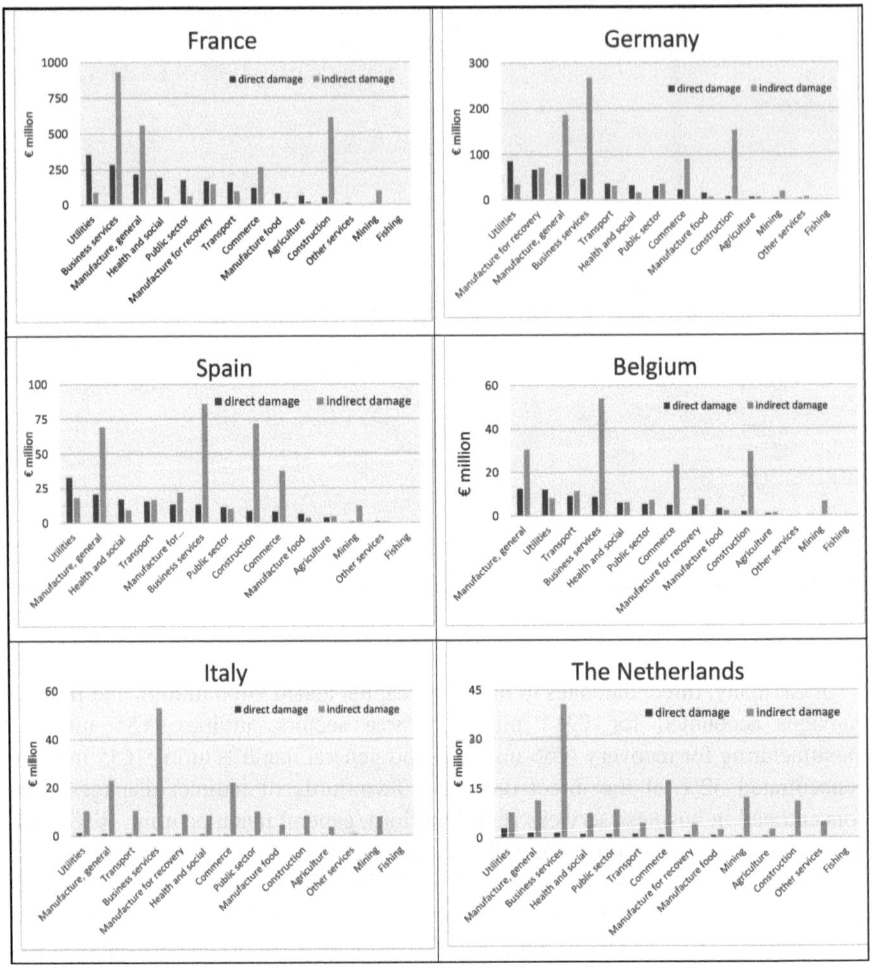

Fig. 4.9 National distribution of direct and indirect damage by industrial sectors. (*Source*: Authors' own elaboration)

European Union, where adaptation policies seek "umbrella" strategies to reduce the climate risk to all the affected regions.

The use of damage functions allows the analysis of different types of disasters, other than floods. The windstorm damage functions were developed in an analogous way to the flood damage functions. While the basic process is the same, additional parameters can be considered, such as wind velocity. This shows that different types of disasters can been analysed through the flood footprint model whenever the damages of a disaster can be expressed as a proportion of industrial capital or labour force productivity.

The results also add to the evidence that indirect damages account for a considerable proportion of the total costs of a disaster. For the Xynthia windstorm, the indirect damages represented 53.3% of the total damages. This also reinforces the results of other researches (Hallegatte 2008; Koks et al. 2014), indicating that the proportion of indirect damages in the total impact of a disaster increases in direct proportion to the size of the damage.

In summary, the flood footprint model was used to assess the total direct and indirect damages of multiple regions. This improves the understanding of the total effects of a disaster and increases the adaptability of the model to undertake more realistic analyses. The use of damage functions increases the flexibility of the model to consider a wide range of disasters. It also allows the incorporation of research results from flood modelling and other hazards, which create the potential to predict damages for projected future events.

It should be noted that up to this point, the model has not considered interregional trade, which is the main contribution of the last case study.

4.3 Adaptation Benefits: The Case of Blue-Green Infrastructure in Newcastle, UK[5]

This case study of the implementation of blue-green infrastructure (BGI) presents the adaptability and applicability of the flood footprint model within a hybrid method to assess the benefits of strategies for flood risk management. This is possible through the integration of a flood model, a multi-benefits evaluation model based on geographical information systems (GIS), and the application of the flood footprint assessment framework.

This hybrid approach assesses the benefits of applying a hypothetical BGI in the city of Newcastle for six return period events.

For each return period event, the flood model estimates the water depth distribution in the area where a BGI would take place. The GIS-based model estimates the direct costs of the flood. Finally, the flood footprint estimates the indirect costs for the whole city for both BGI and the current grey infrastructure (GI) scenarios. Then the total economic costs (or flood footprint) are estimated for each return period and for each infrastructure scenario. Finally, the economic benefits (or avoided costs) of a BGI are defined for each return period event as the difference of total damages under a GI scenario, minus total damages under a BGI scenario. If damages under a BGI scenario are smaller than damages under a GI scenario, the benefits will be positive.

[5]For a full review of this case study, please refer to Mendoza-Tinoco et al. (2020a).

The results show that direct and indirect damages are lower under BGI for all return periods. They also suggest that the proportion of indirect damages in the flood footprint increases as the intensity of the events increase, and they increase more than proportionately for GI. This suggests that BGI implies benefits for all return periods, and the biggest share of benefits comes from avoided indirect damages for higher return period events.

4.3.1 BGI for Flood Risk Management

Cities are particularly vulnerable to floods due to high proportions of impermeable surfaces and the reliance on predominantly traditional piped GI that interrupts the natural cycle of water. The existing infrastructure for flood risk management is put under pressure during heavy rainfall events and storm surges, increasing the chance of exceedance and consequential flood risk. This situation necessitates adaptation measures with new approaches that integrate urban water and flood risk management while permitting sustainable development of the cities at risk.

Within this context, the Blue-Green Cities (BGC) approach proposes the incorporation of BGI, such as swales, green roofs and walls, raingardens, and wetlands into urban environments to promote the recreation of a more naturally oriented water cycle. The multifunctional nature of BGI suggests that at a strategic level, it may assist diverse policies oriented to the enhancement of flood risk management, climate change adaptation, improvements to the quality of the environment, and citizens' health and well-being (Hoyer et al. 2011).

To evaluate the benefits of BGI over traditional grey strategies for flood risk management, we must define first typical GI strategies to manage flood risk and the associated issues when coping with increasing flood events. GI refers to building infrastructure, such as pavement, roads, and bridges. Regarding flood and water management, typical grey engineering approaches include sewerage mains, tunnels, flood barriers and walls, dam construction, and river defences. However, these options alter the natural water cycle by preventing water infiltration into the subsoil, evapotranspiration, and the natural migration of river channels. Moreover, the heat island effect created by cities may alter air circulation, which also generates alterations in climate and water-cycle patterns.

In contrast, BGI and sustainable drainage systems (SuDS) are able to attenuate, infiltrate, store, and generally slow the flow of water through drainage systems. When in place, BGI reduces the pressure on existing grey infrastructure to transfer and treat storm water, improving the performance of existing piped systems and wastewater treatment plants and reducing the severity of floods (Josh et al. 2011). In addition to the benefits associated with reduced flood damages, BGI also creates a wide range of direct benefits to the environment (e.g. reducing heat, improving water quality and carbon sequestration, improving wildlife and biodiversity) and society (e.g. increasing opportunities for recreation, improved aesthetics, and enhanced health and well-being) (Lawson et al. 2014; O'Donnell et al. 2017).

Owing to the above, the BGC approach represents a promising adaptation option for flood risk management and policies for climate change adaptation, with a potential for delivering multidimensional benefits. However, the development of BGC requires a considerable amount of investment in financial and social resources so that the decision must be based on a sound evaluation of the potential net benefits of different approaches.

Moreover, as the flood framework suggests, the reduction in direct damages caused by flooding through BGI would have positive effects in wider areas beyond the site of intervention, owing to a reduction in indirect damages, as well. These benefits may not necessarily be included in traditional cost-benefit analyses, which suggests that the benefits of BGI may frequently be underestimated, thus reducing opportunities for implementation. Therefore, the economic assessment of the ability of BGI to reduce flood risk would serve as a tangible basis on which investment decisions can be built.

For this purpose, this case study presents the results of a hybrid method that merges a GIS Multiple Benefits Toolbox (MBT) (see Morgan and Fenner 2019) and the flood footprint model to quantify the potential economic benefits (or avoided costs) of flood risk management throughout BGI. The economic benefits assessed here are derived from the reduction in costs from flood damages.

The City of Newcastle was selected as a demonstration case study due to its significant pluvial flood risk and relatively recent inundation events. For instance, in the summer of 2012, the city suffered one of the worst floods in the century. According to the Newcastle City Council, the 2012 summer flooding caused direct damages of £34 million in the city (Newcastle City Council 2013), and the flood footprint assessment estimated that indirect damages represented an additional £44 million burden.

4.3.2 Methodology Rationale

The hybrid approach to assess the potential economic benefits of BGI, derived from flood damage mitigation, consists of three stages. First, the MBT calculates the economic damage of a specific return period event under both BGI and GI scenarios for a specific urban area. This provides direct damages by land use category. Secondly, the results from the MBT are encoded to match the industrial categories in the flood footprint model. This is based on a weighted distribution of the economic activity and the size of the city's economy. Finally, the flood footprint model is regionalised for the targeted economy, and it incorporates the data of the direct damages under each of the infrastructure scenarios. The potential direct and indirect benefits for a given return period event are then considered as the difference of the flood footprint estimations under both infrastructure scenarios.

The model provides results for each category for direct and indirect benefits. The disaggregation of benefits by economic sectors are also determined by this approach.

4.3.3 *Data Gathering and Codification*

The assessment of BGI benefits focuses on the City of Newcastle, and the experiment considers six return period scenarios: 200, 100, 50, 30, 10, and 2 years. The return period refers to the probability that an event of a specific magnitude occurs in that period. For instance, a return period of 200 years could be seen as an event with an occurrence's probability of 1/200 or 0.5% in any year. The bigger the return period, the more intense the event, and the lower the probability of occurrence within a given year.

For the MBT, we only describe the data needed for the assessment of flood damages, leaving aside the rest of the benefits and dimensions that the tool can assess. For that purpose, three sets of data are needed: hazard information, infrastructure in place, and damage functions.

4.3.3.1 Hazard Information

Hazard information includes the spatial distribution of flood depth under both GI and BGI scenarios. This data was taken from the City Catchment Analysis Tool (CityCAT), a hydrodynamic model that is able to assess the effects of BG features on water flows and flood depths (Glenis et al. 2013). The model covered the core urban area marked with red in Fig. 4.10, which includes parts of the wards of Wingrove, Westgate, Osborne, South Jesmond, and North Jesmond.

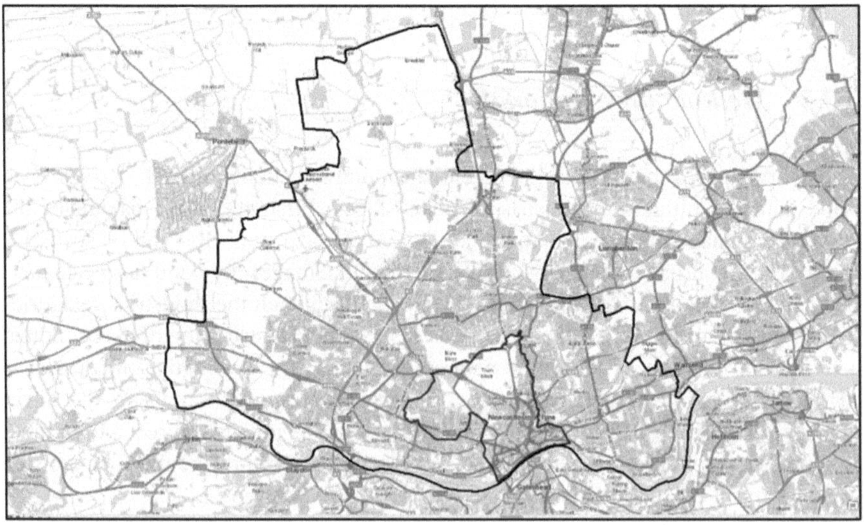

Fig. 4.10 Newcastle upon Tyne Urban core (in red) and the city's administrative boundary (in black). (*Source*: Blue-Green Cities Research Project 2016)

4.3.3.2 Infrastructure Information

The information for the urban infrastructure was gathered using land use distribution and building-type information. The mapping of land use categories was provided in an Ordnance Survey (OS) MasterMap Topographical Layer,[6] while building type information was from the OS Gazetteer Database, supplied by the Newcastle City Council (Blue Green Cities Research Project 2016). MasterMap identifies eight land use categories: residential high density, residential low density, commercial, industrial, mines/construction, recreation, nature, and water. For its part, 104 building type categories are identified in the Gazetteer database, e.g. road, building commercial offices, building residential dwellings, terraces, and railways.

To create the BGI scenario, a hypothetical selection of BGI was added to areas in the city. In Wingrove, a residential area to the northwest of its urban core, all gardens, were designated as greenspace, additional greenspace was added to public areas (equivalent to raingardens), and all pavements and back alleys were designated as permeable paving. Hypothetical BGI interventions were also added around Newcastle University (permeable paving and green roofs) and along streets in the urban core. These include Northumberland Street and John Dobson Streets (green roofs, small (2 × 2 m) swales, permeable paving and street trees), and St James' Boulevard (a large swale along the length of the road and permeable paving) (Blue Green Cities Research Project 2016; Morgan and Fenner 2019). The flood inundation damages were then calculated using the MBT for the reference case (no additional BGI) and BGI scenario. The flood depth for each building and other types of urban infrastructure was assigned and linked to a land use category.

4.3.3.3 Damage Functions

Finally, damage functions were used to calculate a monetary value for the flood damage for the different return periods. These damage functions integrate information on flood depth, type of building, and land use. Each land use has its own depth damage curve which ranges from £88/m^2 for nature to £3385/m^2 for residential high density category for a 3 m deep flood (the maximum depth considered) (Morgan and Fenner 2019).

This information constitutes the basis for constructing the event account vector (EAV) for the flood footprint model, although it must be encoded first to match the categories of the economic sectors in the flood footprint model. The flood footprint model requires two sets of data: economic data about the affected region and information about the disaster. A monthly time scale is used for the temporal analysis, and the sectoral disaggregation uses 46 economic sectors.

[6] https://www.ordnancesurvey.co.uk/business-and-government/products/topography-layer.html

4.3.3.4 Economic Data for Flood Footprint Model

The economic data includes information on capital stock, final demand, employment, and inter-industrial transactions. All the information has been either collected or regionalised at the city level, and in monetary terms, the values are in millions of pounds (£million) at 2009 prices.

Capital stock data is only available at the national level. The regionalisation consisted of obtaining the productivity of each sector at the national level and then adjusting by the city's output, assuming the same productivity as the national average. The regional dwelling capital is the proportion of housing in the region multiplied by the national dwelling capital. For the city of Newcastle, this accounts for 0.54%.

The categories for final demand (households, governments, capital, imports, and exports) were obtained from the UK-Multisectoral Dynamic Model (MDM), by Cambridge Econometrics Ltd.[7] This is a macro-econometric model used to analyse and forecast environmental, energy, and economic data for the 12 regions in the UK. The model provides the data for the Northeast region and for 46 industrial sectors.

To regionalise the data at the city scale, we used employment data, which gives details at the city scale for 18 economic activities. This data was obtained from the 2011 Census by the Office of National Statistics (ONS).[8] To match the sectoral disaggregation with 46 sectors in the MDM to the rest of the data, a weighted distribution was followed based on both national employment and the value-added data from the MDM.

For inter-industrial transactions data, a regionalised matrix of technical coefficients had to be derived from the national IO tables owing to the lack of regional tables. For this purpose, we follow a standard statistical technique in IO modelling, the Augmented Flegg Location Quotients (AFLQ) to obtain the regional IO coefficient matrix for the city of Newcastle upon Tyne. This technique seeks to correct the national technical coefficients to depict regional technology, given the regional economic structure (Flegg and Webber 2000; Miller and Blair 2009; Romero et al. 2012). The transactions' values are obtained later by multiplying the regionalised matrix of technical coefficients by the regional output.

4.3.3.5 Disaster Data

This data is given by the MBT as the monetary value of damages based on flood depth by building type. The data is then allocated to either residential damage or an economic sector to determine the damage to the industrial capital. The proportion of damages to industrial capital is then disclosed in the elements of the EAV.

---

[7] http://www.camecon.com/how/mdm-e3-model/

[8] https://www.ons.gov.uk/employmentandlabourmarket/peoplenotinwork/economicinactivity/adhocs/005609ct05822011censuseconomicactivity

Labour constraints were modelled as a proportion of the number of flooded houses multiplied by the average number of working people per household. Additionally, commuting delays were proportionally related to damage in the transport sectors. A sensitivity analysis was also conducted on this parameter to assure robust results.

4.3.4 The Model's Results

The results of the MBT analysis show that one of the advantages of BGI is the reduction of water depth in all flooding scenarios and, in consequence, the reduction of associated direct damages. This implies that BGI brings potential economic benefits (or avoided damages) in flood risk management.

The calculations show that direct and indirect damages are both lower under BGI scenarios when compared with GI scenarios. The difference of damages between GI and BGI scenarios represents the economic benefits (or the avoided costs) of BGI, for each return period event.

In Fig. 4.11, the proportions of direct (in grey) and indirect (in blue) damages for the 12 scenarios are illustrated, where G = grey Infrastructure and BG = blue-green Infrastructure. It shows the shares of residential and industrial direct damages and indirect damages. The indirect damages increase more than proportionally as the intensity of the flood increases. Consequently, the indirect damages do so, as well. It is also notable that indirect damages are relatively insignificant for events with a short return period. However, it is in the 200-year return period event where the indirect damages become the major share of the damages within the flood footprint.

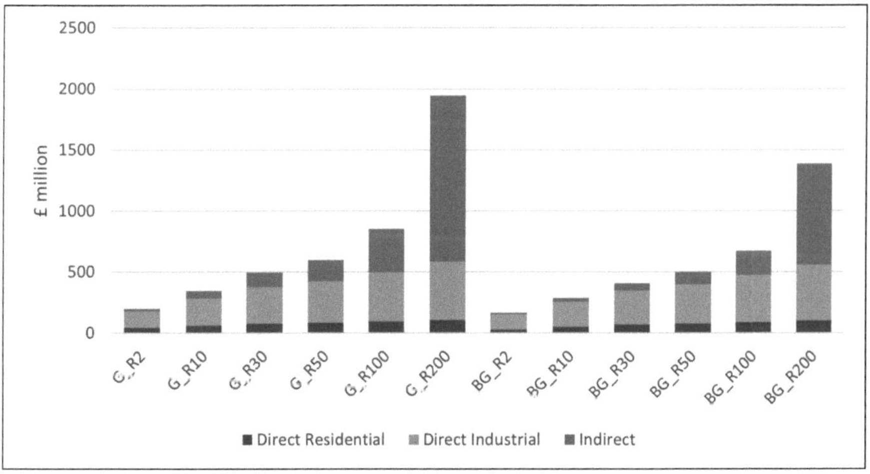

Fig. 4.11 Flood footprint for grey infrastructure and blue-green infrastructure. (*Source*: Authors' own elaboration)

It is notorious that residential damages represent in all cases a small proportion of the direct damages, which remains relatively constant, around 20%.

Regarding indirect damages, they account for a share that goes from 10% to 70% in GI scenarios, while the proportion of indirect damages for BGI scenarios runs from 9% to 60%. This indicates that BGI not only helps in reducing direct damages from a flooding event; indirect damages as proportion of total flood footprint are also reduced.

4.3.4.1 BGI Benefits

As mentioned before, the benefits of BGI are considered as the reduction in total damages under BGI infrastructure scenario vs. the current situation of GI.

The estimations of direct damages from the MBT show a decrease (in relative terms) in the difference between GI scenarios and the BGI scenarios for all return period events. This difference goes from 30% damage reduction between GI and BGI scenarios for the 2-year return period to a difference of just 5% between GI and BGI scenarios for the 200-year return period. However, the story is different for the indirect damages. The percentage change of differences of indirect damages between GI and BGI scenarios increases from 25% in the 2-year return period event to reach a peak of 50% in the 30-year return period event. Then, the proportion of the differences decreases until 39% for the 200-year return period event. However, the proportional differences are always bigger for indirect damages than for direct damages.

Figure 4.12 shows the total benefits (or avoided costs) for the BGI scenario over the GI scenario. The direct "benefits", or the avoided direct costs, remain relatively constant for all return periods (in absolute terms), accounting for around £25 million. The story is different for the indirect benefits, or avoided indirect costs, as they experience a huge increase from £5 million in the 2-year return period, up to

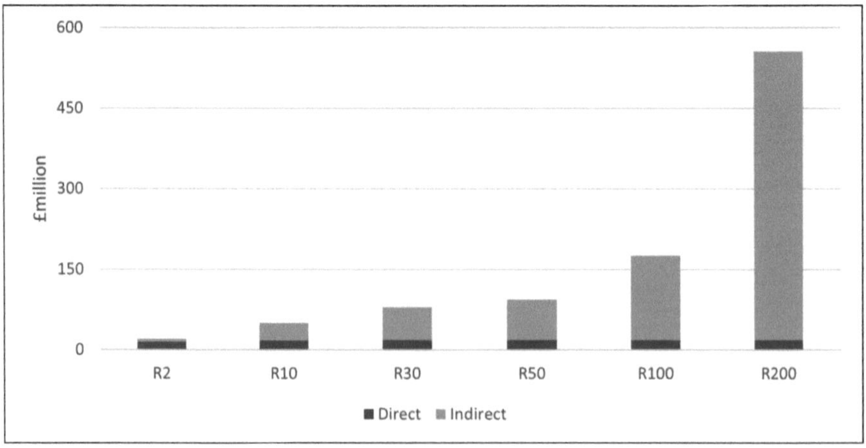

Fig. 4.12 BGI benefits (avoided direct and indirect costs). (*Source*: Authors' own elaboration)

£537 million for the 200-year return period. In relative terms, the share of indirect benefits goes from 14% of the total benefits (for the 2-year return period) up to the 96% of the total benefits (for the 200-year return period). Even if these results are biased by the data generated by the MBT, they reinforce the idea that indirect damages will contribute more to the flood footprint as the intensity of the flood increases, affecting critical infrastructure and consequently triggering major disruptions in the economy.

4.3.4.2 Sectoral Distribution of Benefits

Figure 4.13a–f depicts the distribution of the benefits by industry for each of the return periods. Note that the sectoral distribution is very similar among the different scenarios for each category (indirect and direct benefits) as this depends mostly on the economic structure, which does not change over the different return period events. The different scale for each of the charts should be noted.

The direct benefits concentrate more in those sectors that would be directly benefited from a reduction in flood waters. This occurs more in those sectors that have a bigger proportion of built infrastructure as part of the capital stock, as is the case of manufacturing, utilities, and the transport sectors. In the case of indirect "benefits", they concentrate in the manufacturing and utilities sectors. Other industries that indirectly benefit from avoided damages are those included in the financial and professional sectors. This result has been found in other case studies, as these sectors are highly dependent on the functioning of those sectors related with infrastructure, such as the transport and utilities sectors.

The sectoral analysis depicts the potential damages to specific industries and highlights the hot spots where *more attention should be put to increase the benefits of BGI.*

4.3.5 Summary

This case study presented a hybrid and novel methodology to assess the total economic benefits of a given strategy for flood risk management. The novelty of the approach rests in a consistent integration of flood inundation modelling with the GIS modelling, which links and encodes the results from flood inundation modelling into economic information for impact assessments. This allows the evaluation of the total avoided costs (which here we define as economic benefits) of implementing BGI as a flood risk management strategy.

The data presented here shows that the incorporation of BGI is a viable option to help mitigate damages related to flood risk, potential climate change, and weather-related disasters within a city's environment.

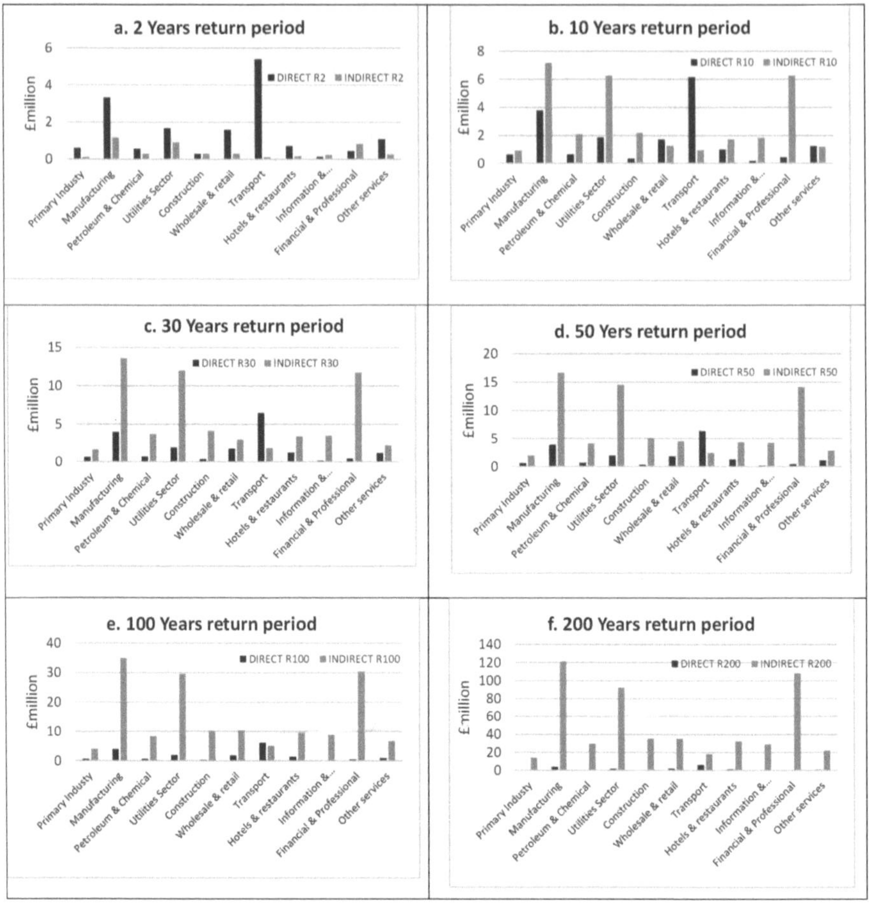

Fig. 4.13 BGI benefits by industry. (*Source*: Authors' own elaboration)

This approach confirms the potential benefits of BGI, not just confined to the area where the assets are built but to wider economic networks. These results show that indirect benefits may be strongly allocated to sectors that are not directly protected by BGI but depend on the appropriate functioning of other sectors under flooding and aftermath circumstances.

4.4 MFFA: Projected Case for Rotterdam, the Netherlands

The purpose of this section is to bring an empirical application of the MFFA to a flooding case in Rotterdam in 2011. As shown in Chap. 2, the MFFA is an extension of the flood footprint model, used to analyse, in addition to the regional direct and indirect costs, the indirect costs to regions that are economically interconnected with the impacted region. Chapter 3 shows the application and results of the MFFA model to a projected flooding scenario in the city of Rotterdam, the Netherlands. Its economic importance, not just for the Netherlands but also for all Europe, and the susceptibility of the area to flooding events make it a relevant case study upon which to apply the MFFA in a multiregional context.

The case study benefited from the data provided within the project "Bottom-up Climate Adaptation Strategies towards a Sustainable Europe (BASE)"[9] for the European Commission with the Grant Agreement No. 308337, which is part of the broader Collaborative project (IP) FP7-ENV-2012-two-stage, Subsidy for Environment (including climate change). This project provided for the analysis of a projected disaster that incorporates a forecast on future climate change and a forecast on the socioeconomic development in the city of Rotterdam, the Netherlands. The chapter shows how the consequences of a disaster in a city affect the national economy and how these disruptions propagate worldwide through its economic interconnections.

4.4.1 Contextual Information of Rotterdam

4.4.1.1 General Information

Rotterdam is one of the most densely populated areas in the Netherlands, with 1.6 million inhabitants in an area of 1130 km^2. It is also one of the most important economic cities in the country and in Europe, as it hosts the largest port on the continent, which is the tenth largest in the world. The city of Rotterdam is located on the delta of the Rhine-Meuse-Scheldt River, in the Midwestern Netherlands. Due to these characteristics, climate change implies an increasing flood risk as a result of the expected sea level rise and the increase in frequency of severe rainfall events (Jeuken et al. 2013). Figure 4.14 shows the location of Rotterdam in relation to the Rhine-Meuse-Scheldt delta and the location of the 24 municipalities that constitute the wider economic area of analysis in this section.

These socioeconomic and geographical characteristics give rise to climate change risk in four areas. The first area at risk is identified as the foreshores of the river Rhine, where major harbour areas are located. Flooding in this area would cause shortages of imports to the city, but also to the country and to Europe as a whole. The second risk hotspot is located behind the flood defences, where most urban activities take place, such as houses, businesses, real estate, etc. This puts the life of the civilian population at risk, and it would cause business interruptions during a flood. The third area of risk is related to interruptions in critical infrastructure behind the flooding defences, such as hospitals, power stations, roads, water treatment plants, etc. Flooding adaptation strategies are urgent in this area, as the functioning and

[9]BASE (2016) project website: http://base-adaptation.eu/

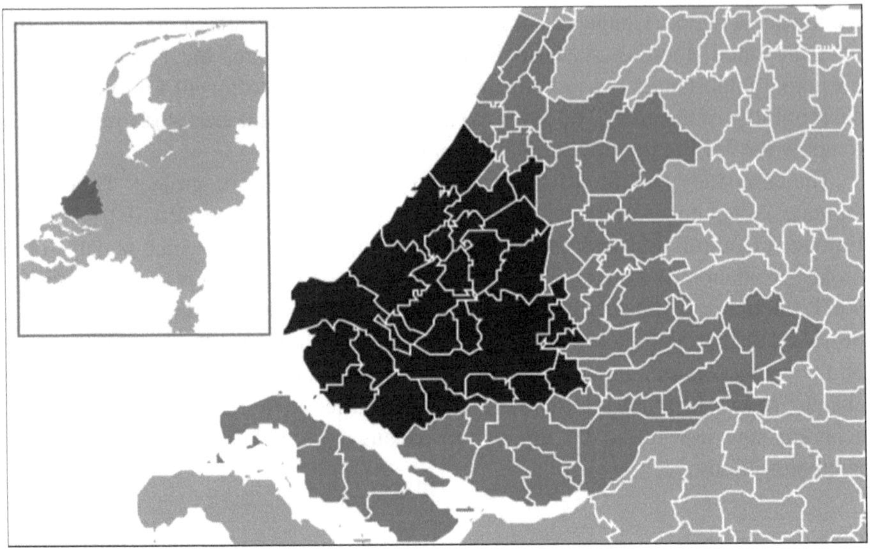

Fig. 4.14 Location of the metropolitan area of Rotterdam. (*Source*: Commons Wikimedia. https://commons.wikimedia.org/wiki/File:Metropoolregio_Rotterdam_Den_Haag_(Rotterdam_The_Hague_Metropolitan_Area).svg)

survival of the socioeconomic system depend on this infrastructure during a disaster aftermath. Finally, the fourth area at risk is the agricultural and rural structures, i.e. lands bordering the urban areas (BASE 2016; Delta Programme Commissioner 2017).

To cope with climate change risk, the city government has implemented major adaptation strategies focused on reinforcing the prime flooding defence system from the river tributaries in the metropolitan area. The system comprises the main water system and the urban water system. The first includes flooding defences such as dikes, storm surge barriers, pumping, and drainage. While the former involves the sewage system, there are also local retention possibilities in parks, squares, and on roofs and improvements to urban water management, in general.

The goal of the adaptation strategies is to provide sufficient flood prevention in the metropolitan area of Rotterdam for future decades, given the expected increase in river discharge due to climate change and the risks that could compromise its socioeconomic development (Delta Programme Commissioner 2017).

4.4.1.2 Historical Flood Risk Context

The western area of the Netherlands, where Rotterdam is located, has been historically prone to flooding events. The worst flooding that the city has experienced dates to 1953 when the Rhine-Meuse-Scheldt delta overflowed in the south of Rotterdam causing a major disaster that resulted in the unfortunate loss of 1836 lives in the Netherlands. After the event, the government decided to construct the delta flooding protection system called Dutch Delta Works, which includes a series of dykes, levees, storm surge barriers, dams, and sluices. Recent flooding includes the events of 2006, during which the city experienced record precipitation levels, accumulating 200 mm within a month. This led to severe flood damage in the Rotterdam metropolitan area. Generally, it should be considered that rainfall events in winter are especially intense, increasing the flood risk during those months. At the time of this book's editing, a catastrophic summer rainfall affected a wide region of Europe, especially Germany, Belgium, and the Netherlands.

The main climate change risk for Rotterdam is sea level rise. During the last century, the North Sea rose 200 mm, with a growth rate of 3 mm per year between 1993 and 2014. The combined effects of climate change and rapid urban development have exacerbated the risk by a factor of 7. Even without climate change, the growth of urban settlements in areas vulnerable to flooding would has increased the level of risk.

These circumstances led to the creation of the Delta Programme in 2010 by the Dutch Parliament to provide adaptation strategies to ensure the resilience of the country during this century. Rotterdam is an essential part of this programme, and the case study here is bounded by the general objectives of that programme (BASE 2016).

4.4.1.3 Urban Planning Context

Located in the delta of the Rhine-Meuse River, life in Rotterdam has been centred on its harbour since its beginnings. Later, industrialisation brought an economic boost to the city as a result of increased commerce through its harbour, until the city centre suffered extensive bombing during the Second World War. However, post-war reconstruction gave rise to new economic growth, repositioning Rotterdam as one of the largest ports in the world.

However, economic development came with important developments from a flood risk perspective, with renewed investment in flood defences, but with a concurrent increase in socioeconomic risk, owing to changes in population density and economic activity intensity (BASE 2016).

4.4.1.4 Institutional Context

The responsibility for adaptation policies regarding flood risk management fall upon the government at different levels. The river tributaries and seashores are mainly the responsibility of the national government, while the responsibility of the urban water system mainly falls on the municipality, alongside partial participation of local boards. Other stakeholders, such as the port authority, civil organisations, and/or large companies, may influence decisions regarding the state of the system. Lastly, the effectiveness of public adaptation policy may be influenced by citizen actions (BASE 2016; Jeuken et al. 2013; Rotterdam Climate Initiative 2014).

4.4.2 *The Data*

Rotterdam was chosen as the case study to apply the MFFA due to the susceptibility of the city to flooding, given the geographical and meteorological circumstances and the increased risks because of projected extreme climate events and socioeconomic development. The data to conduct the MFFA analysis is organised into three sets: (a) monetary information about a disaster's destruction, (b) information on the economic infrastructure, and, in this case, (c) its commercial networks.

4.4.2.1 Disaster Information

The information on flooding projections and damages is provided by the Deltares Research Institute.[10] The flood projection is an average of several future scenarios for Rotterdam developed within the Flood Risk in the Netherlands (Veiligheid Nederland in Kaart – VNK2) project.[11] In general, the project analyses and provides an estimation on flood risk in the Netherlands. The scenarios consist of a range of future climate projections combined with a range of socioeconomic scenarios. In general, the climate scenarios run from moderate to severe climate change projections, while the socioeconomic scenarios range from low to high socioeconomic development estimations (VNK2 project office 2012). The climate scenarios are in line with the projections RCP6.5 and RCP8.5 described in the 5th Assessment Report of the (IPCC 2013). The main foreseeable consequence of climate change in these scenarios related to the flood footprint analysis is an increase in flood risk attributable to higher mean river discharges, increased surface flooding, and problems in sewage as the result of extreme rainfall events.

The estimation of a flood's direct damages under the climate-socioeconomic scenarios is based on information from the *Hoogwater Informatie Systeem*, within its *damage and victims'* module (*Schade en Slachtoffer Module.* HIS-SSM). The HIS-SSM system translates the flooding projection of a specific return period event into direct economic cost using depth damage functions (BASE 2016).

The data for the MFFA in Rotterdam considers a 1:10,000-year return period flood for the described average projection of future climate-socioeconomic scenarios. The estimations of damages consider a combined outline with both sides of the river flooded based on multiple breach locations of the levee. As data from the HIS-SSM is for the year 2000, the values are updated based on information in the Dutch project *Flood Protection for the 21st Century* (in Dutch: Waterveiligheid 21e eeuw, WV21).[12]

---

[10]Deltares Institute: https://www.deltares.nl/en/

[11]VKN2 project: https://www.helpdeskwater.nl/onderwerpen/waterveiligheid/programma'-projecten/veiligheid-nederland/english/flood-risk-the/

[12]WV21: https://www.helpdeskwater.nl/onderwerpen/water-ruimte/klimaat/factsheets/waterveilighe id-21e/

The experiment was considered for 2011, due to information availability. The projected direct costs are provided in US$ millions at 2011 prices, for 49 categories of physical assets, such as roads, airports, urban areas, etc. Using a concordance matrix, the information on direct damages is distributed among 35 industrial sectors to match with the economic information in the MRIO tables.

4.4.2.2 Economic Information

The main source of economic data is the World Input-Output Database[13] (WIOD) (Timmer et al. 2015). The WIOD provides a time series of a world input-output table (WIOT), with data available for the years 1995–2014. The WIOT used in this case study is for 2011, as this matches in time with most of the disaster data. The WIOT contains information for 40 countries (which includes the 27 EU member states and 13 other countries), including a "Rest of the World" (RoW) region.

The table is a compendium of national IO tables constructed by the national accounts interlinked by the international trade with intermediate and final demand. All national tables include 35 industry sectors, following the International Standard Industrial Classification (SIC) of All Economic Activities Rev.3, by the United Nations Statistical Commission (UNSD 2014). Owing to this, the inter-regional matrices are squared matrices with a range of 35 (industries). The WIOT also provides the information of final demand by the region and industry of origin, as well as the region and the category of final consumption. The categories of final consumption include households' final consumption, final consumption by non-profit organisations, government expenditure, gross fixed capital formation, and changes in inventories.

Regarding intermediate demand, when the information in the WIOT is read row-wise for a specific industry (i) in a specific region (r), it depicts the product needs from industry i from region r that are used as inputs for production in all industries in all regions. In other words, the typical element $[z_{ij}^{rs}]$ of the multiregional inter-industrial transactions, Z^R, indicates that the amount of product z that is produced by industry i in region r is going to be used by industry j in region s. For final demand, the typical element $[f_{i,k}^{rs}]$ tells us the amount of product f that is produced in industry i in region r that is demanded in region s to be consumed in the final demand category k. In other words, it explicitly discloses the destiny of exports when the region of destiny is different from the region of origin.

When the table is read column-wise, it provides information on the input requirements of industry j for products of other sectors, from local and external regions, i.e. the element $\left[z_{ij}^{rs}\right]$ indicates the amount of input z from industry i produced in region r that is needed in industry j in region s to generate the production of industry j in region s, x_j^s. It also includes the payments for the productive factors (or the VA)

[13] WIOD: http://www.wiod.org/new_site/data.htm

and other transactions of production, such as taxes and subsidies. For the case of final demand, the tables explicitly disclose the information about the origin of imports for final consumption. Thus, element $[f_{i,k}^{rs}]$ indicates the final demand of products in the category k in the region s that comes from industry i in region r.

The section of the socioeconomic accounts of the WIOD also provides information on capital stock and employment for the same classification of sectors and regions as in the WIOT.

4.4.2.3 Economic Data for Rotterdam

For the Rotterdam case study, to account for damages at the city level, the AFLQ regionalisation method to regionalise the IO tables was applied to obtain the regional IO tables. The economic information to assess the city's economic size was obtained from the statistical office of the EU, Eurostat.[14] This includes information on gross value added (GVA) and employment by industry at the NUTS 2 level.[15] It should be noted that the NUTS2 information is for the region Zuid-Holland (South Holland), which incorporates the city of Rotterdam. This data was used for the industry distribution of intermediate and final demand. The industry aggregation in this dataset is for 14 industrial sectors, so a concordance matrix was used to match the 35-industry disaggregation in the WIOD.

4.4.3 Results of the Multiregional Flood Footprint Analysis

This section presents the results of applying the MFFA model to a projected flood event in Rotterdam.

4.4.3.1 Direct and Indirect Damage

Figure 4.15 shows the distribution of costs in two dimensions: the type of costs (direct or indirect) and the region (national or international).

According to the analysis, the flood footprint of the projected event accounts for US$13.1 billion in total, which, for comparative purposes, represents over 1% of the Netherlands' GDP for the year 2011. Direct costs account for US$8 billion (ca. 61% of the Flood Footprint), from which US$3.6 billion are for residential damages, while US$4.4 billion are for industrial damages.

---

[14]Eurostat: http://ec.europa.eu/eurostat/web/main/home

[15]"The NUTS classification (Nomenclature of territorial units for statistics) is a hierarchical system for dividing up the economic territory of the EU and the UK for the purpose of: NUTS 2: basic regions for the application of regional policies".

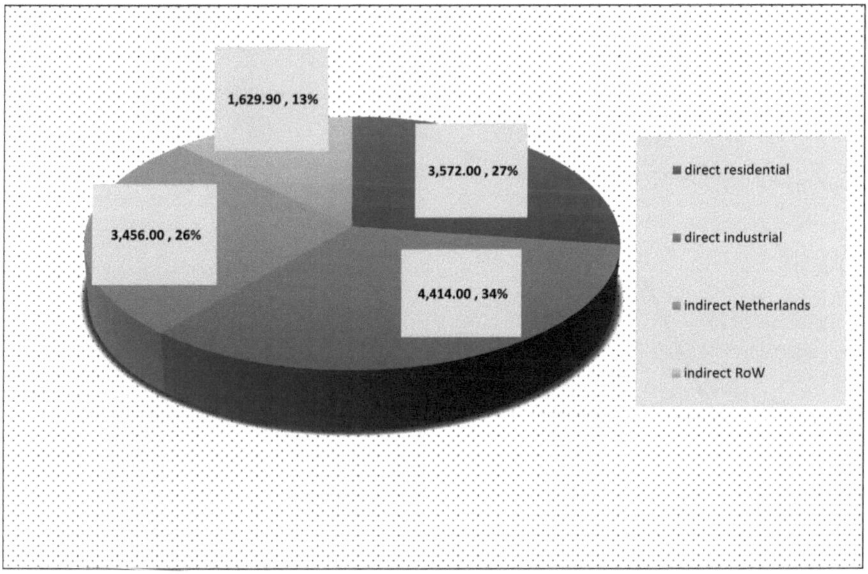

Fig. 4.15 Multiregional flood footprint (US$ million). (*Source*: Authors' own elaboration)

Indirect costs (missed production due to physical damage to industrial and infrastructure capital) represent US$5.1 billion (ca. 39% of the flood footprint). Considering the regional allocation of the indirect damages, US$3.5 billion (ca. 68% of indirect costs) is production lost to the Netherlands' economy. The impact of the flood spills over into other economies, causing a loss of US$1.6 billion (ca. 32% of indirect damage). The ratio of total direct costs to total indirect costs is 1: 0.6, i.e. for each dollar of damage to physical assets, there is an additional 0.6 dollar lost in indirect costs across the Netherlands and the rest of the world.

The impact on other economies through international trade is also considerable. This represents over 12% of the entire flood footprint. It should be noted that the direct costs to Rotterdam are expressed as costs for the Netherlands, as the interregional links in the WIOT data are given at the national level. The regional and industrial distribution of the indirect costs to other economies provides insight into vulnerable links in the international value chain.

4.4.3.2 Recovery Path

Regarding the dynamics and time for economic recovery, Fig. 4.16 shows the overall flood footprint recovery curve. This is certainly influenced by the model's design, although it corroborates the literature which suggests a fast recovery in the first months in the aftermath of a disaster (when resources from emergency plans and international aid are allocated for reconstruction), but which slows down when

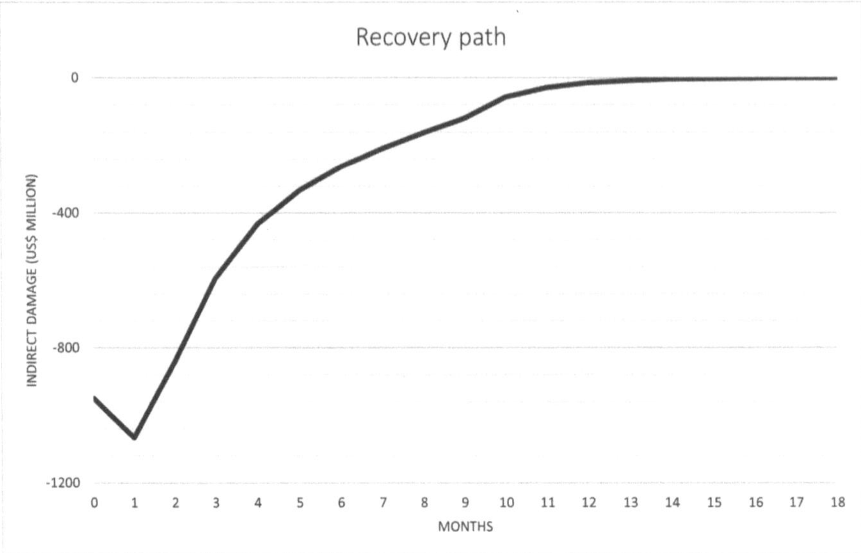

Fig. 4.16 Recovery path. (*Source*: Authors' own elaboration)

approaching the pre-disaster level. It can be noted that even when the model predicts a recovery of 18 months, production is at 98% of the pre-disaster level after the first year of recovery. The remainder of the recovery time allows market imbalances to readjust.

It is important to note that 1 month after the disaster, there is an additional decrease in productivity. As the indirect damage in month zero represents the productivity decrease associated with the direct damage, which only affects the national economy, the additional decrease in production is explained by the loss of productivity outside the Netherlands. This fact reinforces the relevance of the multiregional evaluation of the flood footprint in considering the broader damages from a flooding event that spread out through economic interconnectedness.

4.4.3.3 Regional Distribution

One of the main advantages of a multiregional analysis is the disaggregation of the damage expansion by country. Figure 4.17 shows the regional distribution of indirect costs in the countries most affected. The distribution of these damages is correlated with the trade relations of the Netherlands with other countries and the relative importance of the affected sectors in the international value chain. The cost to the *Rest of the World* regions is the summation of the indirect costs in the remaining 154 countries of the world. The five most damaged countries represent 16% of the total indirect costs and 50% of the indirect costs outside the Netherlands.

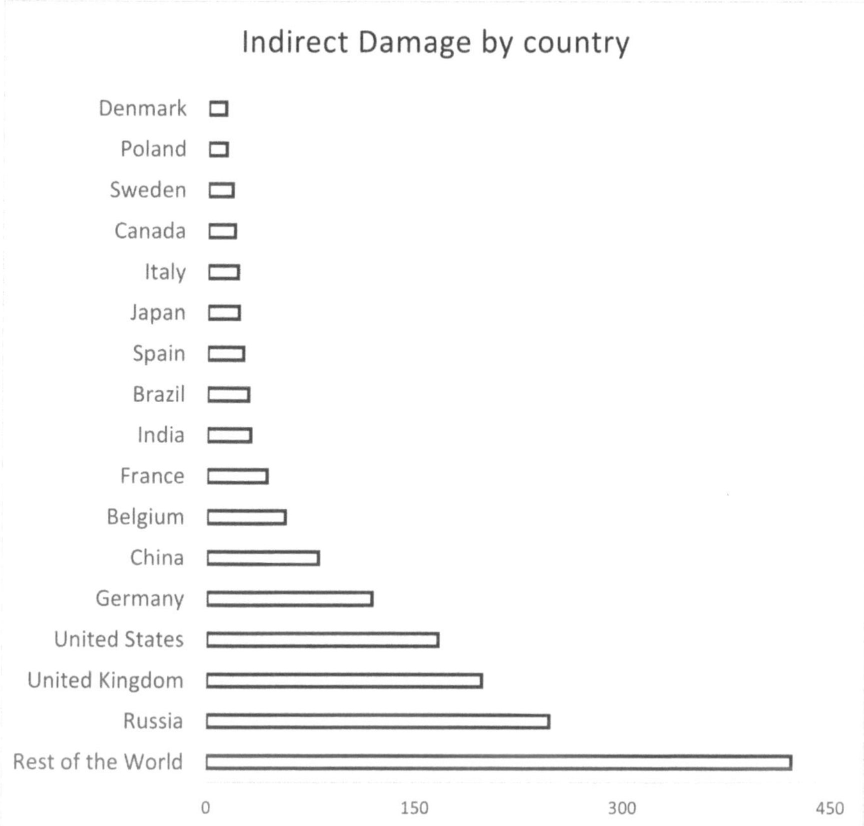

Fig. 4.17 Indirect damage by country (US$ million). (*Source*: Authors' own elaboration)

4.4.3.4 Sectoral Distribution

Finally, Fig. 4.18 shows the sectoral distribution of both industrial direct and indirect costs in the Netherlands. In general, the indirect costs within the Netherlands maintain a ratio of 1:0.8 to the industrial costs incurred in Rotterdam.

The sector most affected by direct flooding impacts is the financial intermediation sector, accounting for US$573 million (ca. 13% of direct damage), followed by food, beverages, and tobacco, coke, refined petroleum and nuclear fuel, and construction sectors, with the damages being over US$300 million.

Regarding indirect costs, it is again the financial intermediation industry which contributes the most to the damage, with US$417 million (ca. 12% of indirect damages within the Netherlands). The other three most affected sectors are real estate activities (US$395 million), machinery and equipment rental and other businesses (US$362 million), and wholesale trade and commission trade industries (US $328 million), which together account for over 30% of indirect costs in the Netherlands.

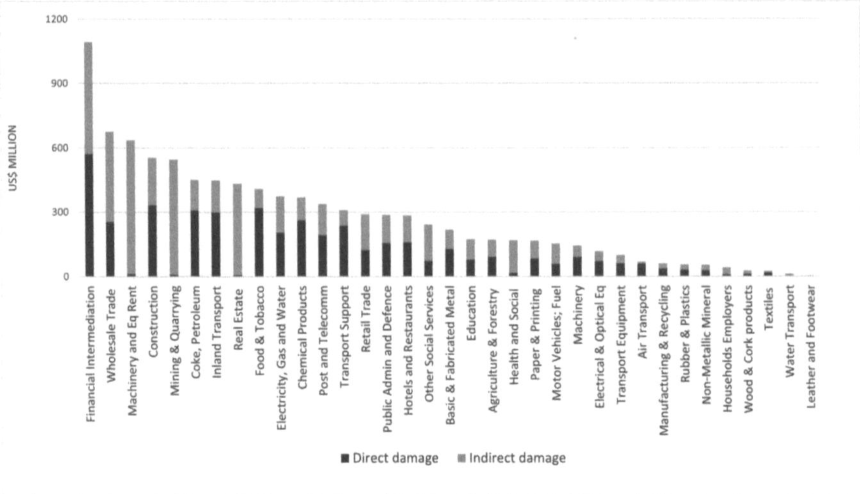

Fig. 4.18 Flood footprint in the Netherlands. (*Source*: Authors' own elaboration)

It is notable that the distribution of indirect costs is grouped mostly in businesses and professional industries, which account for over 50% of the indirect costs in the Netherlands.

4.4.4 Summary

This section presented the application of the MFFA to a disaster scenario. The projected flood scenario in Rotterdam offered the perfect case study, considering climate change and socioeconomic development, to assess the consequences of a major flood. This is due to the flood risk imposed on the region by climate change and due to the relevance of the city's economy to the national economy and wider economic networks, mainly in the European Union.

Once again, the MFFA took advantage of depth damage functions, which is becoming the standard practice in the assessment of flood damages (Moel and Aerts 2011). This allows for the economic impact assessment of future scenarios and allows the consideration of different variables such as economic growth, socioeconomic development, climate change, etc. This makes the MFFA a useful tool for the evaluation of the consequences of extreme climate events related to climate change.

Regarding the modelling extensions, the MFFA model constitutes an important contribution to the improved understanding of the costs of disasters, as it accounts for the economic effects occurring beyond the impacted regions. The transmission mechanisms of the effects from the affected region to the rest of the world are modelled as the reduction of inter-industrial inputs that the non-flooded regions use from the flooded region, i.e. it accounts for the backward effects of constraints in intermediate demand. Due to the way in which the mechanisms of transmission of the effects are modelled, it is expected to have effects in the same direction, i.e. economic losses in the flooded region would trigger economic losses in connected regions. It must be noted, however, that the MFFA model needs further development, and one direction is to consider the effects of imports, which have been shown to bring economic benefits in terms of employment and higher demand to those regions supplying the inputs for reconstruction and final demand that cannot be supplied internally in the flooded region (Hallegatte 2008).

The analysis reveals the relevance of economic interconnectedness and how damages from disasters in a region can spill over into several regions. This should be taken into consideration in adaptation policy planning, especially when generating integrated adaptation policies across different countries. In climate change economics, it is generally argued that mitigation of climate change should entail a global strategy, while adaptation to the consequences of climate change is seen more as a local problem. The type of analysis presented in this chapter offers evidence to question if adaptation to climate change should be local, as the successful adaptation strategies in one region (or reducing the costs of flooding in the case presented here) would benefit wider economic networks. In summary, a multiregional strategy for adaptation policies would decrease the potential damage in highly interconnected economies.

Chapter 5
Concluding Remarks

5.1 Contribution to Knowledge

A useful methodology is proposed to assess the economic costs from physical damages arising from a disaster to understand how the economic shock is transmitted and propagated to wider economic systems and social networks generating additional indirect economic costs. Important ripple effects caused by disasters have not been sufficiently researched in the past. Methodological developments are necessary to improve this research issue. This book has focused on contributing to a fuller understanding of the wider economic impacts of disasters, especially of the regional distribution of their indirect impacts.

This purpose is twofold: (a) to calculate the direct costs to each economic sector or industry based on the information provided by different estimation methods for flood damage to physical assets, such as the use of financial reports or depth damage functions and flood modelling, and (b) to estimate secondary effects, considering the economic mechanisms that affect production in industries and regions economically linked with sectors in the affected region. This second purpose is the most challenging.

5.2 Key Method Development

This methodology has been tested and its usefulness demonstrated when applied to diverse case studies based on diverse scenarios.

The final version of the MFFA is a model that considers flood damages to physical assets in infrastructure, industrial capital, and residential capital. It also accounts for disruptions to the labour force that are experienced during a disaster. Moreover, the model can incorporate behavioural changes in final consumption.

© The Author(s), under exclusive license to Springer Nature Switzerland AG 2023

D. Mendoza-Tinoco et al., *Multiregional Flood Footprint Analysis*, SpringerBriefs in Economics, https://doi.org/10.1007/978-3-031-29728-1_5

Therefore, the model evaluates the production disruptions to linked economic sectors, both within and outside the affected region. From this point of view, the model provides a dynamic recovery route map that the economy can follow towards its recovery. In summary, it provides a general picture of the total multiregional economic effects that result from a disaster.

This methodology offers novelty in three main ways: extension, applicability, and adaptability.

5.2.1 Extension

The methodology incorporates methodological elements to consider diverse aspects of economic impact analysis that had not previously been incorporated into an integrated model. These comprise the multiregional dimension of the analysis, dynamic-time recovery, the effects from labour disruptions, residential damages, the effects of behavioural change on final consumption, and the transition from capital investment for recovery to reconstruction of productive capacity.

5.2.2 Applicability

Paralleling each stage of the model's development, a related case study was presented, chosen because of the relevance of the event or the scenario it covered. Most of the case studies related to previous stages of this model's development have already been published in academic journals and are now presented in this book in their final version.

The single-regional model was applied to the analysis of a real event in the past, the 2007 summer floods in the UK (Mendoza-Tinoco et al. 2017), with the analysis being applied to the regions of Yorkshire and the Humber, the areas most affected by the event.

The multiple single-regional analysis was also applied to real past events (the 2009 summer floods in Central Europe and the 2010 Xynthia windstorm), which, in these cases, affected several subnational regions across different countries (Mendoza-Tinoco et al. 2020b).

Finally, the multiregional analysis presented here was applied to a hypothetical case considering future scenarios of climate change and socioeconomic development in the city of Rotterdam, the Netherlands.

5.2.3 *Adaptability*

We distinguish two main directions in which the MFFA can adapt, given the experiences gained from these case studies.

First, the MFFA provides great integration possibilities with engineering flood models, GIS models, depth damage functions, or more traditional reports from damage evaluation in situ. This expands the potential of flood footprint modelling, as flood modelling has experienced rapid development in recent years. Additionally, GIS models can make more accurate estimations of the geographical distribution of damages and, in combination with depth damage functions, provide a more accurate, prompt, and efficient estimation of damages.

Secondly, the MFFA framework has been shown to be adaptable to other purposes. The transferability of the model was demonstrated when applied to other natural hazards in addition to flooding events, as shown in the case of the 2010 Xynthia windstorm. Moreover, the model was applied to assess the benefits of a flood risk management strategy. This is the case study of the evaluation of blue-green infrastructure in the city of Newcastle upon Tyne, UK, as an option to mitigate damage caused by future flooding events (Mendoza-Tinoco et al. 2020a).

5.3 Policy Implications

The MFFA model can be used to support the decision-making of disaster relief plans and resiliency strategies. Important insights can be drawn from the results of the four case studies presented here, including the following two outcomes:

- The proportion of indirect damage over the total economic costs of a disaster (or flood footprint) represents a considerable share that ranges from 9.09% to 69.96% in the several cases where the model was applied. This fact, by itself, justifies the relevance of accounting for the indirect costs of a disaster. The risk of not considering the indirect effects can undermine flood risk management strategy, leaving those industries that are indirectly affected to be exposed to further damages.
- It is notable that direct costs are concentrated in the manufacturing and infrastructure service industries, such as electricity, gas, water, telecommunications, and transport, whereas the indirect costs tend to accumulate in the tertiary industries, such as the financial and other business sectors. This can be explained by two factors. On the one hand, the manufacturing and infrastructure sectors have, in general, more in-built capital stock and equipment; hence, more capital is exposed to damage from floodwaters (or other disasters). On the other hand, business services and other related industries largely rely on infrastructure services, such as the transport and telecom industries. A small failure in infrastructure industries would imply severe production disruptions in businesses and industries.

The MFFA reveals the strong interconnections in modern economies, such that a shock affecting a regional economy will have consequences in its commercial partners. This last point raises the necessity to create multiregional adaptation strategies to reduce the risk of climate change, as the consequences of these changes extend across all economies linked directly or indirectly to the affected region.

5.4 Implications for Stakeholders and Policy Makers

The MFFA identifies the industries most affected by both direct and indirect costs of a disaster. For investing in risk management options for disasters, it is critical to identify the "blind spots" in critical infrastructure and the vulnerable sectors along the economic supply chain and social networks. This, in turn, would allow for sufficient adaptation to damages, transferring knowledge gained from current events to future ones. Adaptation to disaster risk should not be limited to the area likely to suffer direct damages. It also should extend to its socioeconomic networks, and this must be considered to minimise the magnitude and probability of damages cascading to other regions.

At the level of disaster risk mitigation responsibility, the MFFA would also provide an alternative way to allocate financial responsibility for disaster risk mitigation interventions by incorporating the value of all stakeholders' economic capacities on the local/regional/national/international supply chains, based on the "who benefits, who pays" principle. In other words, if a disaster footprint assessment reveals that organisation(s) *x* or *y* benefit in a large way from disaster defence, then alternative management payment schemes could be considered. This could potentially reduce society's financial burden for risk management of disasters and spread the cost between the major stakeholders in the supply chain.

In the international context of climate change, a MFFA could potentially reduce the financial burden and reallocate resources for climate risk management in more vulnerable regions of the world, spreading the cost between major economies in the supply chain that would potentially benefit from climate risk reduction in those more vulnerable regions, a topic related to climate justice that has started to be debated.

At a communication level, the MFFA could be an excellent concept to enhance business and public awareness of the possible damage threatening them and of the total damage a disaster can cause, as well.

5.5 Limitations of the MFFA

The main limitation of MFFA modelling comes from the datasets used. Flood modelling is greatly improving and can deliver very accurate estimations of floodwater depth; however, when translating the flooding characteristics into economic damages, the use of depth flood damages uses average damage values for a generic asset. This creates a degree of uncertainty and bias in the analysis.

The data available on labour and household consumption in the aftermath of a flood is very limited. The former represents a serious source of uncertainty, as the model has high sensitivity to small changes in labour parameters, while variations in the latter do not substantially affect the results.

The multiregional analysis is also limited to a national level analysis, as multiregional tables at the subnational level exist for very few countries.

Other limitations are related to the nature of the subjacent IO model, such as rigidities for input substitutions, and fixed-proportion production functions.

Another limitation in the model is that recovery does not consider an economic growth path, as recovery is considered to have occurred when the economy reaches its pre-disaster conditions.

5.6 Future Research

Although this model has been useful in assessing the economic impact of disasters, there are some aspects which deserve attention to improve and expand the potential of the methodology.

First, the computing capabilities and science advances in understanding climate change effects can provide a damage estimation of a disaster, almost in real time as soon as some parameters of a disaster are known. A "climate risk map" could be developed to help in reducing the vulnerability of and enhancing the resilience of the regions and industries at risk. This would provide a consistent analysis across different cases and would significantly reduce analysis time.

Second, as the frequency of disasters increase, some regions are impacted by a second disaster before their economy has fully recovered from the first one. The intent exists to extend the flood footprint to assess these types of scenarios, as well, incorporating adaptation measures that may reduce the impact of subsequent disasters. A pioneer analysis considering these situations can be found in a study by Zeng and Guan (2020).

Third, since impacted economies take time to recover after a major flooding event, it has been pointed out that their production would have been expected to grow in the absence of the disaster, so the recovery of those economies should aim to reach previously projected future levels of production.

Finally, further research should aim to map climate risk along the global value chain. In climate change economics, the mitigation of climate change is usually seen as a global problem, while adaptation is treated as a local problem. The evidence provided by analyses similar to the MFFA point out the need to develop global adaptation strategies, allocating resources for climate risk management in those vulnerable regions that, if impacted by a disaster, would trigger severe indirect costs to other countries with more resources for adaptation. Therefore, this analysis could be applied to provide evidence and awareness for the need of a global adaptation strategy for damages caused by climate change effects.

References

BASE (2016). Bottom-up climate adaptation strategies towards a sustainable Europe. Case-study: Rotterdam. In E. Commission (Ed.). *Seventh Framework Programme*. Delft, The Netherlands: Deltares.

Batey, P. W. J. and Rose, A. Z. (1990). Extended Input-Output Models: Progress and Potential. *International Regional Science Review*. 13(27). https://doi.org/10.1177/016001769001300103

Blue Green Cities Research Project. (2016). *Delivering and Evaluating Multiple Flood Risk Benefits in Blue-Green Cities*. http://www.bluegreencities.ac.uk/

Bockarjova, M., Steenge, A. and van der Veen, A. (2004). On Direct Estimation of Initial Damage in the Case of a Major Disaster: Derivation of the "Basic Equation". *Disaster Prevention and Management*, 13(4), 330–336.

Cochrane, H. (1997). Economic Impact of a Midwest Earthquake. *NCEER Bulletin*, 11(1), 1–15.

Cochrane, H. (2004). Economic loss: myth and measurement. *Disaster Prevention and Management*, 13(4), 290.

Cole, S. (2003). Protection, Risk and Disaster in Economic Network. In A. van der Veen, A. L. V. Arellano and J. P. Nordvik (Eds.). *In Search of a Common Methodology for Damage Estimation*. Workshop Proceedings, Delft, the Netherlands, Office for Official Publications of the European Communities: Joint NEDIES and University of Twente.

Crowther, K. G. and Haimes, Y. Y. (2010). Development of the Multiregional Inoperability Input-Output Model (MRIIM) for Spatial Explicitness in Preparedness of Interdependent Regions. *Systems Engineering*, 13(1), 28–46.

Crowther, K. G., Haimes, Y. Y. and Taub, G. (2007). Systemic Valuation of Strategic Preparedness Through Application of the Inoperability Input-Output Model with Lessons Learned from Hurricane Katrina. *Risk Analysis*, 27(5), 1345–1364.

Daly, H. (1968). On Economics as a Life Science. *Journal of Political Economy*. 76. 392–406.

Delta Programme Commissioner (2017). *Delta Programme 2017*. Work on the delta: Ministry of Infrastructure and the Environment and the Ministry of Economic Affairs.

Dietzenbacher, E. (1997). In vindication of the Ghosh model: a reinterpretation as a price model. *Journal of Regional Science*, 37(4), 629–651.

Dietzenbacher, E. and Lahr, M. L. (2013). Expanding extractions. *Economic Systems Research*, 25(3), 341–360. https://doi.org/10.1080/09535314.2013.774266

Flegg, A. and Webber, D. (2000). Regional Size, Regional Specialization and the FLQ Formula. *Regional Studies*, 34(6), 563–569.

Galbusera, L. and Giannopoulos, G. (2018). On input-output economic models in disaster impact assessment. *International Journal of Disaster Risk Reduction*, 30 (2018) 186–198.

© The Editor(s) (if applicable) and The Author(s), under exclusive license to Springer Nature Switzerland AG 2023

D. Mendoza-Tinoco et al., *Multiregional Flood Footprint Analysis*, SpringerBriefs in Economics, https://doi.org/10.1007/978-3-031-29728-1

Ghosh, A. (1958). Input-Output Approach in an Allocation System. *Economica, New Series*, 25(97), 58–64.

Glenis, V., McGough, A. S., Kutija, V., Kilsby, C. and Woodman, S. (2013). Flood modelling for cities using Cloud computing. *Journal of Cloud Computing: Advances, Systems and Applications*, 2(1), 1–14.

Gould, K. A., Garcia, M. M. and Remes, J. A. (2016). Beyond "natural-disasters-are-not-natural": The work of state and nature after the 2010 earthquake in Chile. *Journal of Political Ecology*, 23(1), 93–114.

Haimes, Y., Horowitz, B. M., Lambert, J. H., Santos, J. R. and Crowther, K. G. (2005). Inoperability input-output model (IIM) for interdependent infrastructure sectors: theory and methodology. *Journal of Infrastructure Systems*, 11(2), 67–79.

Haimes, Y. and Jiang, P. (2001). Leontief-based model of risk in complex interconnected infrastructures. *Journal of Infrastructure Systems*, 7, 1–12.

Hallegatte, S. (2008). An Adaptive Regional Input-Output Model and its Application to the Assessment of the Economic Cost of Katrina. *Risk Analysis*, 28(3), 779–799.

Hallegatte, S. and Przyluski, V. (2010). The Economics of Natural Disasters. Concepts and Methods. *World Bank Policy Research Working Paper* (5507).

Hoyer, J., Dickhaunt, W., Kronawitter, L. and Weber, B. (2011). *Water Sensitive Urban Design – Principles and Inspiration for Sustainable Stormwater Management in the City of the Future.* Hamburg, Germany: Hafen City Universitat.

IPCC (2013). *Climate Change 2013: The Physical Science Basis. Contribution of Working Group I to the Fifth Assessment Report of the Intergovernmental Panel on Climate Change.* [T.F. Stocker, D. Qin, G.-K. Plattner, M. Tignor, S.K. Allen, J. Boschung, A. Nauels, Y. Xia, V. Bex and P.M. Midgley (eds.)]. Cambridge University Press, Cambridge, United Kingdom and New York, NY, USA.

Israd, W. (1968). On the Linkage of Socio-Economic and Ecological Systems. *Papers of the Regional Science Association*. 21. 79–99

Jeuken, A., N. Slootjes, J. K., Gauderis, J. and Vos, R. (2013). Cost-benefit analysis of flood risk management strategies for the Rhine-Meuse delta. Comprehensive Flood Risk Management, *Research for policy and practice*, 436.

Josh, F., Ashley, L. and Steve, W. (2011). *The Value of Green Infrastructure for Urban Climate Adaptation.* Retrieved from Wasington, D.C., USA: http://dev.cakex.org/sites/default/files/Green_Infrastructure_FINAL.pdf

Koks, E. E., Carrera, L., Jonkeren, O., Aerts, J. C., Husby, T. G., Thissen, M. ... and Mysiak, J. (2016a). Regional disaster impact analysis: comparing input–output and computable general equilibrium models. *Natural Hazards and Earth System Sciences*, 16(8), 1911–1924.

Koks, E. E., Bockarjova, M., de Moel, H. and Aerts, J. C. J. H. (2014). Integrated Direct and Indirect Flood Risk Modelling: Development and Sensitivity Analysis. *Risk Analysis*, 35(5), 882–900. https://doi.org/10.1111/risa.12300

Koks, E. E., Carrera, L., Jonkeren, O., Aerts, J. C. J. H., Husby, T. G., Thissen, M. and Mysiak, J. (2016b). Regional disaster impact analysis: comparing Input-Output and Computable General Equilibrium models. *Natural Hazards and Earth System Sciences*, 3, 7053–7088. https://doi.org/10.5194/nhessd-3-7053-2015

Koks, E. E. and Thissen, M. (2016). A Multiregional Impact Assessment Model for disaster analysis. *Economic Systems Research*, https://doi.org/10.1080/09535314.2016.1232701

Kunz, M., Mühr, B., Kunz-Plapp, T., Daniell, J.E., Khazai, B., Wenzel, F., Vannieuwenhuyse, M., Comes, T., Elmer, F., Schröter, K., Fohringer, J., Münzberg, T., Lucas, C. and Zschau, J. (2013). Investigation of superstorm Sandy 2012 in a multi-disciplinary approach. Natural Hazards Earth System Science, 1, 625–679. https://doi.org/10.5194/nhessd-1-625-2013

Lawson, E., Thorne, C., Ahilan, S., Allen, D., Arthur, S., Everett, G. ... and Wright, N. (2014). Delivering and evaluating the multiple flood risk benefits in Blue-Green Cities; an interdisciplinary approach. *Flood Recovery Innovation and Response*, 184. https://doi.org/10.2495/FRIAR140101

Lazzaroni, S. and van Bergeijk, P. A. (2014). Natural disasters' impact, factors of resilience and development: A meta-analysis of the macroeconomic literature. *Ecological Economics*, 107, 333–346.

Leung, M., Haimes, Y. Y. and Santos, J. R. (2007). Supply- and Output-Side Extensions to the Inoperability Input-Output Model for Interdependent Infrastructures. *Journal of Infrastructure Systems*, 13, 299–310.

Li, J., Crawford-Brown, D., Syddall, M. and Guan, D. (2013). Modelling Imbalanced Economic Recovery following a Natural Disaster using Input-Output Analysis. *Risk Analysis*, 16.

Mendoza-Tinoco, D., Guan, D., Zeng, Z., Xia, Y. and Serrano, A. (2017). Flood Footprint of the 2007 Floods in the UK: The case of the Yorkshire and The Humber region. *Journal of Cleaner Production*, https://doi.org/10.1016/j.jclepro.2017.09.016

Mendoza-Tinoco, D, Guan, D, Fenner, R, Thorne, C. and O'Donnel, E. (2020a). Flood Footprint Modelling to Evaluate the Flood Risk Management Benefits of Blue–Green Infrastructure. In: C. R Thorne (Eds.). *Blue–Green Cities: Integrating urban flood risk management with green infrastructure*. ISBN 978-0-7277-6419-5. ICE Publishing: All rights reserved https://doi.org/10.1680/bgc.64195.133

Mendoza-Tinoco, D., Hu, Y., Zeng, Z., Chalvatzis, K., Zhang, N., Steenge, A. and Guan, D. (2020b). Flood Footprint Assessment: A Multiregional Case of 2009 Central European Floods. *Risk Analysis*. 40(8). https://doi.org/10.1111/risa.13497.

Messner, F., Penin-Rowsell, E., Green, C., Meyer, V., Tunstall, S. and van der Veen, A. (2007). Evaluating flood damages: guidance and recommendations on principles and methods. (Repor No. GOCE-CT-2004-505420). FLOODsite. https://repository.tudelft.nl/islandora/object/uuid:5602db10-274c-40da-953f-34475ded1755/datastream/OBJ/download

Miller, R. E. and Blair, P. D. (2009). *Input Output Analysis: Foundations and Extensions*. (2 ed.). Englewood Cliffs, US: Prentice-Hall.

Moel, H. D. and Aerts, J. C. J. H. (2011). Effect of uncertainty in land use, damage models and inundation depth on flood damage estimates. *Natural Hazards*, 58, 407–425. https://doi.org/10.1007/s11069-010-9675-6

Morgan, M. and Fenner, R. (2019). Spatial evaluation of the multiple benefits of sustainable drainage systems. In *Proceedings of the Institution of Civil Engineers-Water Management* (Vol. 172, No. 1, pp. 39–52). Thomas Telford Ltd.

Newcastle City Council (2013). *Summer 2012 Flooding in Newcastle upon Tyne*. A report on the experiences of residents and non-residential property managers (pp. 25). Newcastle, UK: Newcastle City Council.

O'Donnell, E., Woodhouse, R. and Thorne, C. (2017). Evaluating the multiple benefits of a Newcastle surface water management scheme. *Proceedings of the ICE – Water Management*. https://doi.org/10.1680/jwama.16.00103

Okuyama, Y. (2003). Modelling Spatial Economic Impacts of Disasters: I-O Approaches. In A. van der Veen, A. L. V. Arellano and J. P. Nordvik (Eds.). *In Search of a Common Methodology for Damage Estimation*. Workshop, Delft, Office for Official Publications of the European Communities: Joint NEDIES and University of Twente.

Okuyama, Y. (2004). Modelling spatial economic impacts of an earthquake: input-output approaches. *Disaster Prevention and Management*, 13(4), 297–306.

Okuyama, Y. (2007). Economic Modelling for Disaster Impact Analysis: Past, Present and Future. *Economic Systems Research*, 19(2), 115–124.

Okuyama, Y. (2009). *Critical Review of Methodologies on Disaster Impact Estimation*. Background Paper to the joint World Bank-UN Assessment on the Economics of Disaster Risk Reduction.

Okuyama, Y. and Santos, J. R. (2014). Disaster impact and input–output analysis. *Economic Systems Research*, 26(1), 1–12.

Oosterhaven, J. and Bouwmeester, M. C. (2016). A new approach to modelling the impact of disruptive events. *Journal of Regional Science*, 56(4), 583–595.

Oosterhaven, J. and Többen, J. (2017). Wider economic impacts of heavy flooding in Germany: a non-linear programming approach. *Spatial Economic Analysis*, 12:4, 404–428, https://doi.org/10.1080/17421772.2017.1300680

Park, J. Y. (2009). Application of a Price-Sensitive Supply-Side Input-Output Model to an Examination of the Economic Impacts: The Hurricane Katrina and Rita Disruptions of the U.S. *Oil-Industry. Paper 128.* Non-Published Research Report. Ecological Economics. Retrieved from http://research.create.usc.edu/nonpublished_reports/128

Penning-Rowsell, E., Priest, S., Parker, D., Morris, J., Tunstall, S., Viavattene, C. and Owen, D. (2013). *Flood and Coastal Erosion Risk Management. A Manual for Economic Appraisal.* London and New York: Routledge.

Pitt, M. (2008). The Pitt Review. Learning lessons from the 2007 floods. Cabinet Office, London. Retrieved from http://archive.cabinetoffice.gov.uk/pittreview/_/media/assets/www.cabinetoffice.gov.uk/flooding_review/pitt_review_full%20pdf.pdf

Romanoff, E. and Levine, S. (1981). Anticipatory and Responsive Sequential Interindustry Models. *IEEE Transactions on Systems, Man and Cybernetics*, 1(3), 181–186.

Romero, C. A., Mastronardi, L. J. and Faye, M. J. (2012). Location quotient analysis. The case of Cordoba state. *Munich Personal RePEc Archive* (36997), 27.

Rose, A. (1995). Input-Output Economics and Computable General Equilibrium Models. *Structural Change and Economic Dynamics*, 6(3), 295–304.

Rose, A. (2004). Economic Principles, Issues and Research Priorities in Hazard Loss Estimation. In Y. Okuyama and S. E. Chang (Eds.), *Modelling Spatial and Economic Impacts of Disasters.* Berlin Heidelberg New York: Springer-Verlag.

Rose, A., Cao, Y. and Oladosu, G. (2000). Simulating the economic impacts of climate change in the Mid-Atlantic Region. *Climate Research*, 14, 175–183.

Rotterdam Climate Initiative (2014). *Delta Rotterdam. Connecting water with opportunities. Rotterdam Climate Initiative.* [Molenaar, A. and Gebraad, C.] Baltzer Science Publishers. Water Governance.

Sahin, I. and Yavuz, O. (2015). Econometric Analysis of Natural Disasters' Macro-Economic Impacts: An Analysis on Selected Four OECD Countries. *Journal of Business Economics and Finance,* 4(3).

Santos, J. R. (2006). Inoperability input-output modelling of disruptions to interdependent economic systems. *Systems Engineering*. 9, 1(20–34), https://doi.org/10.1002/sys.20040

Santos, J. R. and Haimes, Y. Y. (2004). Modelling the Demand Reduction Input-Output (I-O). Inoperability due to Terrorism of Interconnected Infrastructures. *Risk Analysis*, 24(6), 1437–1451.

Santos, J. R. and Rehman, A. (2012). Risk-based input-output analysis of hurricane impacts on interdependent regional workforce systems. *Natural Hazards*, 65(1), 391–405.

Steenge, A. E. and Bočkarjova, M. (2007). Thinking about Rigidities and Imbalances in Post-Disaster Economies: An Input-Output Based Proposition. *Economic Systems Research*, 19(2), 2005–2223.

Sun, R., Gao, G., Gong, Z. and Wu, J. (2020). A review of risk analysis methods for natural disasters. *Natural Hazards*, 100(2), 571–593.

Timmer, M. P., Dietzenbacher, E., Los, B., Stehrer, R. and Vries, G. J. d. (2015). An Illustrated User Guide to the World Input–Output Database: The Case of Global Automotive Production. *Review of International Economics*, 23(3), 575–605. https://doi.org/10.1111/roie.12178

Triple E Consulting (2014). Climate extremes. Defining a pilot approach on estimating the direct and indirect impacts on economic activity. In E. Commission (Ed.). *Climate Action*. European Commission: European Commission.

Tukker, A., Poliakov, E., Heijungs, R., Hawkins, T., Neuwahl, F., Rueda-Cantuche, J. M., Giljum, S., Moll, S. Oosterhaven, J. and, Bouwmeester, M. (2008). Towards a Global Multi-Regional Environmentally Extended Input-Output Database. *Ecological Economics* 68(7), 1928–1937, https://doi.org/10.1016/j.ecolecon.2008.11.010

UNSD (2014). *International Standard Industrial Classification of All Economic Activities*, Rev.3. 2016, from https://unstats.un.org/unsd/cr/registry/regcst.asp?Cl=2

Veen, A. V. D. (2004). Disasters and economic damage: macro, meso and micro approaches. *Disaster Prevention and Management*, 13(4), 274–279.

Veen, A. V. D. and Logtmeijer, C. (2003). How Vulnerable are We for Flooding? A GIS Approach. In A. van der Veen, A. L. V. Arellano and J. P. Nordvik (Eds.). *In Search of a Common Methodology for Damage Estimation*. Workshop, Delft, Office for Official Publications of the European Communities: Joint NEDIES and University of Twente

Victor, P. (1972). *Pollution: Economy and Environment*. London: George Allen and Unwin Ltd.

VNK2 Project Office (2012). *Flood risk in The Netherlands*. VNK2: The method in brief. Helpdesk Water.

Xia, Y., Guan, D., Steenge, A. E., Dietzenbacher, E., Meng, J. and Mendoza Tinoco, D. (2019). Assessing the economic impacts of IT service shutdown during the York flood of 2015 in the UK. *Proceedings of the Royal Society A-Mathematical Physical and Engineering Sciences*, 475(2224), [20180871]. https://doi.org/10.1098/rspa.2018.0871

Xu, W., Hong, L., He, L., Wang, S. and Chen, X. (2011). Supply Driven Dynamic Inoperability Input -Output Price Model for Interdependent Infrastructure Systems. *Journal of Infrastructure Systems*, 17, 151–162.

Zeng, Z. and Guan, D. (2020). Methodology and application of flood footprint accounting in a hypothetical multiple two-flood event. *Philosophical Transactions of the Royal Society A*, 378(2168), https://doi.org/10.1098/rsta.2019.0209.

Cochrane, H. (2004). Economic loss: myth and measurement. *Disaster Prevention and Management,* 13(4), 290.

Zhou, L. and Chen, Z. (2021). Are CGE models reliable for disaster impact analyses? *Economic Systems Research*, 33(1), 20–46.

MIX
Papier aus verantwortungsvollen Quellen
Paper from responsible sources
FSC® C105338

If you have any concerns about our products,
you can contact us on
ProductSafety@springernature.com

In case Publisher is established outside the EU,
the EU authorized representative is:
Springer Nature Customer Service Center GmbH
Europaplatz 3, 69115 Heidelberg, Germany

Printed by Libri Plureos GmbH
in Hamburg, Germany